React for Beginners *Build Powerful User Interfaces with Ease*

A Step-by-Step Guide to Mastering React for Front-End Development

MIGUEL FARMER

RAFAEL SANDERS

Table of Content

TABLE OF CONTENTS

INTRODUCTION

React for Beginners: Build Powerful User Interfaces with Ease

Welcome to "React for Beginners: Build Powerful User Interfaces with Ease"!

If you're a web developer or aspiring to become one, mastering **React** is an essential step towards building modern, high-performance web applications. React is one of the most widely used JavaScript libraries for developing interactive user interfaces, enabling you to create fast, scalable, and dynamic web applications. In this book, we will guide you through the process of learning React from the ground up, using simple, real-world examples that you can immediately apply to your own projects.

React's declarative nature and component-based architecture have made it a favorite among developers. Whether you're building a single-page application (SPA) or a complex enterprise-level system, React provides the flexibility and efficiency needed to create responsive and user-friendly applications. This book is designed to take you from a beginner to a proficient React developer, covering everything you need to know, from the basics to advanced techniques.

Who This Book is For

This book is tailored for developers who are:

- **New to React**: If you're just getting started with React, this book will walk you through its key concepts and help you build a solid foundation.
- **Familiar with JavaScript**: If you already have some experience with JavaScript and want to dive deeper into React, this book will help you understand how to use React effectively to create dynamic user interfaces.
- **Looking to Transition to React**: Whether you're familiar with other JavaScript frameworks or libraries, this book will make the transition to React smoother and more intuitive.

Even if you're an experienced developer, this book will provide you with practical examples and best practices to help you refine your skills and build more robust applications.

What You Will Learn

React is a powerful tool for building modern, interactive web applications. But it's not just about knowing the syntax; it's about understanding the core concepts that drive React's efficiency and scalability. In this book, we will explore:

- **React Components**: Learn the fundamental building blocks of React—components. You will understand how to create functional and class components, manage state, and pass data between components using **props**.

- **JSX Syntax**: JSX is a syntax extension that looks similar to HTML but provides more powerful functionality in React. You'll master JSX, including expressions, attributes, and how it fits into the overall React architecture.

- **State and Props**: These are the heart of React. You'll learn how to use state to manage dynamic data and props to pass data between components, enabling you to create interactive, dynamic UIs.

- **Event Handling**: Learn how to handle user interactions like clicks, form submissions, and keyboard events. React's declarative approach to event handling is both intuitive and powerful.

- **React Router**: Explore how to add navigation to your single-page applications with React Router. You'll learn how to manage routes, render different views, and handle user input dynamically.

- **React Hooks**: Modern React development leverages hooks like **useState** and **useEffect** to add state and side effects to functional components. This book will introduce you to these powerful tools and show you how they simplify component logic.

- **Component Lifecycle**: Understanding the lifecycle of a component is crucial to managing side effects, setting up data fetching, and optimizing performance. You'll explore the **component lifecycle** methods in class components and hooks in functional components.

- **Handling Forms and Validation**: Forms are a critical part of web applications. In this book, you will learn how to manage form data, validate user input, and submit data to the backend.

- **Error Boundaries**: Learn how to handle errors in React gracefully using **error boundaries** to prevent crashes and provide a better user experience.

- **Testing React Components**: You'll gain a hands-on understanding of **unit testing** and **integration testing** using **Jest** and **React Testing Library**, which will help you write bug-free and reliable code.

- **Deployment**: Learn how to deploy your React applications to the web using platforms like **Netlify**, **Heroku**, and **AWS**, ensuring that your apps are production-ready and accessible to users.

Why This Book is Different

Unlike other React tutorials, this book takes a **step-by-step approach**, introducing each concept in a simple and easy-to-understand manner. Each chapter includes **real-world examples**, so you can see how React is used in practical applications. This hands-on approach will help you build a solid foundation in React development, and by the end of the book, you will be able to create your own React applications with confidence.

Structure of the Book

This book is divided into **six parts** to guide you through the React learning process:

1. **Getting Started with React**: Understand the fundamentals of React, how it fits into modern web development, and how to set up your development environment.
2. **Core React Concepts**: Dive deep into components, JSX, state, props, and event handling to build interactive UIs.
3. **Advanced React Concepts**: Learn about hooks, context, and error boundaries to manage complex state and lifecycle behaviors in your apps.
4. **Working with External Data**: Explore how to fetch data from APIs, manage forms, and handle CRUD operations with React.
5. **State Management and Optimization**: Understand how to optimize your app's performance, manage global state with Redux, and improve efficiency.
6. **Building Full-Stack Applications**: Combine everything you've learned to create a full-stack React app, deploy it, and make it ready for production.

Each chapter builds upon the previous one, gradually increasing in complexity. We'll conclude with a **final project**, where you will build and deploy a complete full-stack application, integrating everything you've learned throughout the book.

Real-World Examples and Exercises

Throughout the book, you will find **real-world examples** that demonstrate how to apply React in practical scenarios. Whether it's handling form submissions, managing state, or optimizing performance, these examples provide a hands-on approach to learning. You will also find **exercises** at the end of each chapter to test your understanding and reinforce the concepts covered.

Conclusion

By the end of this book, you will have a **comprehensive understanding of React** and its ecosystem, empowering you to create fast, efficient, and dynamic web applications. Whether you're working on a personal project, a startup's product, or enterprise-level applications, the skills you gain here will be invaluable.

React has transformed the way we build web applications, and with this book, you'll be able to leverage its full potential. Let's get started, and together, we'll build powerful user interfaces with ease. Happy coding!

CHAPTER 1

INTRODUCTION TO REACT AND WHY IT'S SO POPULAR

React has taken the front-end development world by storm, becoming one of the most popular libraries for building user interfaces (UIs). Whether you are a new developer or an experienced professional, understanding React is crucial for building modern, dynamic, and performant web applications. In this chapter, we will dive into what React is, why it has gained such popularity, and how it is used in modern web development. We will also explore real-world use cases where React shines, from small applications to large-scale, enterprise-level apps.

1.1 What is React and Why It's One of the Most Widely Used Libraries for Building UIs?

At its core, **React** is a **JavaScript library** for building user interfaces, particularly single-page applications where you need a fast and interactive user experience. It was developed by **Facebook** and released as an open-source project in 2013. Over the years, React has grown in popularity and has become a go-to solution for front-end developers due to its efficiency, flexibility, and developer-friendly features.

Key features that make React popular:

- **Component-Based Architecture**: React encourages building UIs by creating reusable components, which makes it easier to manage and scale large applications. Each component encapsulates its own structure, logic, and style, making it self-contained and independent from other parts of the application.
- **Declarative Syntax**: React uses a declarative approach to building UIs. This means that you describe the UI in terms of the state of your components, and React will automatically update the UI when the state changes. This is different from the imperative approach, where you explicitly manipulate the DOM.
- **Virtual DOM**: React uses a Virtual DOM, which is an in-memory representation of the actual DOM. When the state of a component changes, React first updates the Virtual DOM, compares it to the previous version, and then only updates the real DOM with the changes. This results in **faster rendering** and improved performance.
- **Unidirectional Data Flow**: In React, data flows in a single direction, which makes it easier to understand and manage how data moves through the application. The

14

parent component can pass data down to child components through **props**, and child components can communicate back to parents via **callbacks**.

1.2 Key Benefits of React in Front-End Development

React offers several compelling advantages that make it a preferred choice for front-end development:

- **Performance**: React's use of the Virtual DOM significantly boosts the performance of web applications, particularly when handling complex UIs with a lot of interactive elements. By minimizing direct interactions with the actual DOM, React ensures that only necessary updates are made, which reduces the number of expensive DOM operations.
- **Reusable Components**: React's component-based structure allows developers to build **modular** and **reusable** UI elements. These components can be shared across different parts of an application or even between different projects. This leads to cleaner, more maintainable code.
- **Rich Ecosystem**: React has a vibrant ecosystem with a rich set of libraries, tools, and extensions. From state management libraries like **Redux** and **Context API** to

router libraries like **React Router**, React's ecosystem provides everything you need to build sophisticated applications. Additionally, there are numerous third-party libraries and tools that extend React's capabilities, such as **Material-UI** for design components or **Axios** for making API requests.

- **Strong Community Support**: Since React is open-source and has a large developer community, there is a wealth of learning resources, tutorials, and documentation available. If you face an issue, chances are someone has already faced it and shared a solution. This support ecosystem is a huge benefit for both beginner and experienced developers.

- **Flexibility and Integration**: React can be easily integrated with other libraries and frameworks. While React itself handles the view layer of your application, it can be paired with other technologies like **Node.js** for the backend or **GraphQL** for API queries. React also integrates well with traditional frameworks like **Django** or **Ruby on Rails**, making it a flexible choice for a wide range of applications.

- **Fast Learning Curve**: React's simple and declarative syntax allows new developers to quickly pick it up. With its **JSX** syntax, React components look similar to HTML, making it familiar to developers with basic web development knowledge. The learning curve is relatively flat, and you can start building applications quickly.

1.3 Understanding React's Role in Modern Web Development

React plays a significant role in modern web development by simplifying the process of building dynamic, responsive, and user-friendly web applications. Here's a closer look at how React fits into the modern development stack:

- **Single-Page Applications (SPAs)**: React is especially well-suited for building **single-page applications** where content is dynamically updated without reloading the page. This is made possible by React's declarative rendering and Virtual DOM, ensuring smooth and fast updates when the user interacts with the application.

- **Componentization in Modern Development**: The rise of **component-based architecture** has fundamentally changed the way developers build applications. React popularized this approach, making it easier to create modular, reusable components that encapsulate both UI and logic. This leads to faster development cycles, easier testing, and better maintainability.

- **React for Mobile Development**: React's influence extends beyond web applications. With the **React Native** framework, you can use the same React knowledge to build mobile applications for iOS and Android. React Native shares many of the same concepts as React, which makes it easy to transition from web to mobile development without having to learn entirely new technologies.

- **Server-Side Rendering (SSR) and Static Site Generation (SSG)**: React's popularity has also contributed to the rise of **server-side rendering (SSR)** and **static site generation (SSG)** in web development. Tools like **Next.js** and **Gatsby** allow developers to use React for building **SEO-friendly** static websites and server-rendered apps, bridging the gap between static sites and dynamic applications.

- **React and Progressive Web Apps (PWAs)**: React is a powerful choice for building **Progressive Web Apps** (PWAs) that combine the best features of both web and mobile applications. PWAs offer offline support, push notifications, and a mobile-first experience, and React's efficiency makes it an ideal choice for building such apps.

1.4 Real-World Use Cases: From Small Applications to Enterprise-Level Apps

React's flexibility and power make it suitable for a wide range of use cases, from simple applications to large-scale, enterprise-level platforms. Let's explore some real-world examples of React in action:

- **Small-Scale Applications**: React is perfect for building **simple, interactive applications** like to-do lists, weather apps, or blog dashboards. Its fast rendering, ease of use, and modularity make it ideal for quickly building and deploying small web applications.

  Example: A to-do list application that allows users to add, edit, and delete tasks. Using React's component-based structure, you can easily create reusable components for each task, while state management ensures that the list updates dynamically as users interact with it.

- **E-Commerce Platforms**: For more complex applications, such as **e-commerce platforms**, React shines in handling dynamic content, product listings, shopping carts, and user interactions. With React, you can build scalable and maintainable e-commerce websites that provide smooth, responsive user experiences.

  Example: An e-commerce website where users can browse products, add them to a cart, and complete a checkout process. React's state management system ensures that the shopping cart updates in real time as users add or remove items.

- **Social Media Platforms**: React is used extensively in social media platforms due to its ability to manage real-time updates and dynamic content. The architecture of React makes it easy to display user-generated content such as posts, comments, likes, and notifications, while maintaining a fast and responsive UI.

Example: A social media application that allows users to post status updates, like posts, and comment on content. React's **unidirectional data flow** helps ensure that the UI stays in sync with the underlying data.

- **Enterprise-Level Applications**: Large-scale applications such as **enterprise resource planning (ERP)** systems, **customer relationship management (CRM)** software, and **analytics dashboards** benefit from React's scalability, performance, and ability to manage complex user interactions and large datasets.

Example: A data analytics dashboard where users can filter and analyze large sets of data in real-time. React's **Virtual DOM** helps ensure smooth performance even when dealing with a lot of dynamic content.

Conclusion

In this chapter, we have introduced **React** as a powerful library for building user interfaces. React's component-based architecture, performance optimizations, and flexibility make it a top choice for modern web development. Whether you're building small-scale applications or large enterprise systems, React's ability to create fast, dynamic, and interactive UIs ensures that it will remain a central tool in the web developer's toolkit.

In the next chapter, we will dive into **setting up your development environment**, installing React, and building your first simple React application. Let's take the first step towards mastering React!

CHAPTER 2

SETTING UP YOUR DEVELOPMENT ENVIRONMENT

In this chapter, we will walk through the steps to set up your development environment for building React applications. Setting up a proper environment is crucial for making development smooth and efficient. We will begin by installing the necessary software, setting up React with **create-react-app**, and learning about the basic structure of a React app. Finally, we'll run our first React application and explore the **React DevTools** for debugging.

2.1 Installing Node.js and npm (Node Package Manager)

Before you can start building React applications, you need to install **Node.js** and **npm** (Node Package Manager). These tools are essential for managing your React project dependencies and running scripts.

- **Node.js** is a JavaScript runtime environment that allows you to run JavaScript on your server (or your local machine). It's required to run React and handle various development tasks.

- **npm** is the default package manager for Node.js. It helps you install and manage packages (dependencies) that are required for your project.

Installing Node.js and npm

1. Go to the official Node.js website: https://nodejs.org.
2. Download the **LTS (Long-Term Support)** version. This version is stable and recommended for most users.
3. Run the installer and follow the on-screen instructions. The installer will automatically install both **Node.js** and **npm** on your system.
4. Once the installation is complete, you can verify that Node.js and npm were successfully installed by running the following commands in your terminal or command prompt:

```bash

node -v
npm -v
```

- If the installation was successful, you'll see the version numbers for both Node.js and npm.

2.2 Setting Up a Development Environment with create-react-app

Now that Node.js and npm are installed, the next step is to set up your React project. React provides a tool called **create-react-app** that simplifies the process of creating a new React application. It sets up the basic structure of a React app and installs all the necessary dependencies, allowing you to start building right away.

Using create-react-app

1. Open your terminal (or command prompt).
2. To create a new React app, run the following command:

bash

```
npx create-react-app my-first-app
```

- `npx` is a tool that comes with npm, and it runs packages without installing them globally.
- `create-react-app` is the package that sets up a new React project.
- `my-first-app` is the name of the folder where your new app will be created. You can replace this with any name you prefer.

3. Once the project setup is complete, you'll see a folder named `my-first-app` containing the files and

24

directories for your React app. Navigate to the project folder:

```bash
```

```
cd my-first-app
```

2.3 Introduction to the Structure of a React App

After creating a React app with **create-react-app**, you'll notice the following basic folder structure:

```graphql
```

```
my-first-app/
├── node_modules/          # Directory containing
project dependencies (automatically created by
npm)
├── public/                # Public files that
are not processed by Webpack
|    └── index.html        # The main HTML file
that loads your React app
├── src/                   # Source code of the
React application
|    ├── App.css           # Styles for the App
component
|    ├── App.js            # The root component
of your React app
```

25

```
|     ├── index.css          # Global styles
|     ├── index.js           # The entry point of
your React app (where React renders the app)
├── package.json            # Configuration file
for npm, including dependencies and scripts
├── README.md               # A README file with
basic instructions
```

- **public/index.html**: This is the main HTML file. It contains a `div` with the ID `root`, where the React app will be rendered.
- **src/index.js**: This is the entry point for your React application. React starts here and renders the entire app inside the `root` div.
- **src/App.js**: This is the root component of your React app. You can think of it as the starting point for your UI. It's where you'll start building your UI components.
- **package.json**: This file contains metadata about your project, including the project name, dependencies, and scripts (e.g., `npm start` for running your app).

2.4 Running Your First React App

Now that we've set up the development environment and understand the structure of the app, let's run your first React app.

1. In your terminal, ensure you are in the `my-first-app` directory and run the following command to start the development server:

```bash
```

```
npm start
```

2. This command starts the React development server and opens your default web browser, navigating to http://localhost:3000, where you'll see your first React app running.

What happens when you run `npm start`?

- The development server compiles your React app and serves it at `localhost:3000`.
- React uses **hot reloading**, meaning that whenever you make changes to the code, the browser automatically refreshes to reflect those changes without needing to reload the page manually.

2.5 Exploring the React DevTools for Debugging

One of the best ways to debug and inspect React applications is using **React DevTools**. This is a browser extension that provides an interface for inspecting and interacting with React components in real-time.

Installing React DevTools

1. **For Google Chrome**:
   o Go to the Chrome Web Store and search for **React Developer Tools**.
   o Click **Add to Chrome** to install the extension.
   o Once installed, you will see a "React" tab in the Chrome DevTools panel when inspecting your React application.
2. **For Firefox**:
   o Go to the Firefox Add-ons site and search for **React Developer Tools**.
   o Click **Add to Firefox** to install the extension.

Using React DevTools

Once installed, you can open the DevTools panel in your browser and click on the **React tab** to see a tree structure of your components. This gives you a deeper look at your React components, including their current state and props, making it easier to debug issues.

- **Components View**: View and interact with the component tree of your React app.

- **Profiler**: Analyze the performance of your app and identify slow rendering components.
- **Inspect State and Props**: See the current state and props of each component in real time.

React DevTools helps you visualize how your components are structured, inspect their data, and track re-renders, which is essential for optimizing performance and troubleshooting issues.

Conclusion

In this chapter, we set up a **React development environment** by installing **Node.js** and **npm**, and used **create-react-app** to generate a new React project. We explored the basic **folder structure** of a React app and ran our first React app on the development server. Finally, we introduced **React DevTools**, a powerful tool for debugging and inspecting your React application.

In the next chapter, we'll dive deeper into the **basics of React components**, which are the foundation of every React application. You'll learn how to create and organize components, pass data between them, and start building the structure of your app. Let's continue this exciting journey into the world of React!

CHAPTER 3

UNDERSTANDING THE BASICS OF REACT COMPONENTS

In this chapter, we'll dive into the heart of React: **components**. Components are the building blocks of every React application. Whether you're building a simple to-do list app or a large-scale web platform, understanding how to create and use components is essential. We'll explore the different types of components in React, how they manage state, and when to use them. By the end of this chapter, you'll understand the fundamental concepts of React components and be able to create a simple React app with ease.

3.1 What Are Components and Why They Are the Building Blocks of React Apps?

At the core of React lies the idea of **components**. Simply put, a **component** is a **reusable building block** of a React application. Components can be thought of as JavaScript functions or classes that return a section of the user interface (UI). React components are responsible for managing **UI structure**, **interactivity**, and **presentation**.

- **Component-Based Architecture**: React encourages breaking down the UI into smaller, reusable components. This allows developers to work on individual pieces of the app without interfering with the rest of the system.
- **Separation of Concerns**: Components handle their own state and logic, ensuring a clean separation between the structure of the app (UI) and the logic that powers it (state, behavior).

For example, in a to-do list app, you could have separate components for:

- A to-do item.
- The task list.
- The form to add new tasks.

Each of these components can be defined independently and combined to build the entire app.

3.2 Stateless vs. Stateful Components

React components can be categorized based on whether or not they manage their own state:

- **Stateless Components** (also called **Presentational Components**): These components **do not manage their own state**. They simply receive data (props) and render the UI accordingly. They focus only on displaying content.

Example: A component that just renders a greeting message could be considered a stateless component.

jsx

```
function Greeting(props) {
  return <h1>Hello, {props.name}!</h1>;
}
```

In this example, `Greeting` doesn't maintain any internal state. It just receives the `name` prop and displays it.

- **Stateful Components** (also called **Container Components**): These components manage their own **state** and control how data is rendered and updated in the UI. Stateful components are responsible for handling user interactions, data fetching, and changing the UI based on the state.

Example: A counter component that increments a number is stateful because it maintains the count as part of its internal state.

32

```jsx
jsx

class Counter extends React.Component {
  constructor(props) {
    super(props);
    this.state = { count: 0 };
  }

  increment = () => {
    this.setState({            count:
this.state.count + 1 });
  };

  render() {
    return (
      <div>
        <p>Count: {this.state.count}</p>
        <button
onClick={this.increment}>Increment</butto
n>
      </div>
    );
  }
}
```

In the above example, the `Counter` component holds its state in the `this.state` object. When the button is clicked, the state updates, and the component re-renders with the new count.

33

3.3 Functional vs. Class Components: When to Use Each

React components can be written as either **functional components** or **class components**. Both types are used for rendering UI, but the way they handle state and lifecycle methods differs.

- **Functional Components**:

    A **functional component** is simply a JavaScript function that returns UI elements. Prior to React 16.8, functional components were stateless and did not have access to state or lifecycle methods. However, with the introduction of **React Hooks**, functional components can now manage state and side effects (like fetching data), making them a powerful alternative to class components.

    Example of a Functional Component:

    jsx

    ```jsx
    function HelloWorld() {
      return <h1>Hello, World!</h1>;
    }
    ```

When to use: Use functional components when you need simple, presentational components, or when you want to take advantage of **React Hooks** for state management and side effects.

- **Class Components**:

A **class component** is a JavaScript class that extends React.Component and has access to **state** and **lifecycle methods** (methods that run at specific points in the component's life cycle, such as componentDidMount or componentWillUnmount).

Example of a Class Component:

jsx

```
class HelloWorld extends React.Component {
  render() {
    return <h1>Hello, World!</h1>;
  }
}
```

When to use: Class components were traditionally used when state or lifecycle methods were needed. However, with the advent of React Hooks, the need for class components has decreased in favor of functional components.

3.4 Real-World Example: Creating a Simple "Hello World" Component

Let's create a basic **"Hello World"** component to see how React components work in action.

Stateless Functional Component Example

This is the simplest type of React component, which only takes props and renders UI.

jsx

```
import React from 'react';

function HelloWorld(props) {
  return <h1>Hello, {props.name}!</h1>;
}


export default HelloWorld;
```

In this example:

- The component is a **stateless functional component**.
- It accepts a `name` prop and renders a greeting.

Using the Component

To use the `HelloWorld` component in an app, you can import it into another component, such as the main `App` component.

```jsx
import React from 'react';
import HelloWorld from './HelloWorld';

function App() {
  return (
    <div>
      <HelloWorld name="React Developer" />
    </div>
  );
}

export default App;
```

Explanation:

- The `HelloWorld` component is rendered inside the `App` component, and the `name` prop is passed to it.
- When you run this code, it will display the text: **"Hello, React Developer!"**

37

Stateful Class Component Example

Let's modify the example and make the component **stateful** by adding a button to change the greeting.

```jsx
import React, { Component } from 'react';

class HelloWorld extends Component {
  constructor(props) {
    super(props);
    this.state = {
      name: 'React Developer',
    };
  }

  changeName = () => {
    this.setState({      name:        'JavaScript
Enthusiast' });
  };

  render() {
    return (
      <div>
        <h1>Hello, {this.state.name}!</h1>
        <button onClick={this.changeName}>Change
Name</button>
      </div>
```

```
    );
  }
}
```

```
export default HelloWorld;
```

In this example:

- The component is now **stateful** and uses the `this.state` object to store the `name`.
- The `changeName` method updates the state when the button is clicked, causing the component to re-render with the new name.

Using the Stateful Component

```jsx
jsx

import React from 'react';
import HelloWorld from './HelloWorld';

function App() {
  return (
    <div>
      <HelloWorld />
    </div>
  );
}

export default App;
```

Explanation:

- When the app starts, the greeting will be "Hello, React Developer!"
- Clicking the "Change Name" button will update the greeting to "Hello, JavaScript Enthusiast!" by updating the state.

Conclusion

In this chapter, we've explored the foundational concept of **React components**. Components are the core building blocks of any React application, and understanding them is crucial to becoming proficient with React.

- **Stateless components** are ideal for simple UI elements that don't need to manage state.
- **Stateful components** are essential when you need to manage and update state within a component.
- We also explored the difference between **functional components** and **class components**, and learned how to use both to create React applications.

Now that you understand the basics of React components, you are ready to begin building more dynamic, interactive UIs. In the next chapter, we will explore **JSX**, React's powerful syntax extension that allows you to write HTML inside your JavaScript code. Let's continue building on this foundation!

CHAPTER 4

JSX – THE SYNTAX EXTENSION FOR JAVASCRIPT

In this chapter, we will dive into **JSX**, one of the most distinctive features of React. JSX allows developers to write HTML-like syntax directly within JavaScript, making React components more intuitive and readable. Although JSX looks similar to HTML, it is much more powerful and flexible. We will explore what JSX is, why it's used in React, and how to effectively use it to create dynamic user interfaces.

4.1 What is JSX and Why It's Used in React?

JSX stands for **JavaScript XML**. It is a **syntax extension** for JavaScript that allows you to write HTML elements and components in a way that is embedded within JavaScript code. JSX makes it easier to visualize the structure of a React component and simplifies the process of building UI components by combining the power of JavaScript with the familiarity of HTML.

- **JSX and React**: In React, **components** are responsible for rendering the UI, and JSX is used to define how these components should render. When you write JSX, React will convert it into JavaScript code that creates virtual DOM elements. This makes the process of creating dynamic UIs more intuitive and less error-prone.

Why use JSX?

- **Declarative Syntax**: JSX allows developers to write components in a declarative manner, where the UI is described in terms of the state of the component. This makes the code easier to understand and manage.
- **Readability**: JSX allows for a more readable and understandable representation of the UI compared to traditional JavaScript code, where you would need to manually create HTML elements with `document.createElement()` or other methods.
- **Performance**: React compiles JSX into efficient JavaScript code, ensuring high-performance rendering when the application state changes.

Here's an example of JSX in a React component:

```jsx
import React from 'react';
```

```
function Greeting() {
  return <h1>Hello, World!</h1>;
}

export default Greeting;
```

In the example above:

- The `Greeting` component returns JSX (`<h1>Hello, World!</h1>`).
- This JSX is transformed by React into JavaScript code that creates an `h1` element in the DOM.

4.2 How JSX Looks Like HTML But Is More Powerful

At first glance, JSX looks almost identical to HTML. However, there are several differences that make JSX more powerful and flexible for React development.

Here are some important differences between JSX and HTML:

- **JSX is not HTML**: While JSX resembles HTML, it's not exactly the same. For example, in JSX, class attributes are written as `className` (instead of `class` in HTML) because `class` is a reserved keyword in JavaScript.

Incorrect in JSX:

```
html
```

```
<div class="container">
```

Correct in JSX:

```
jsx
```

```
<div className="container">
```

- **JSX Requires a Root Element**: A JSX expression must return a single root element. If you need to return multiple elements, you can wrap them inside a `div`, or use `React.Fragment` (or shorthand `<>...</>`).

Incorrect JSX:

```
jsx
```

```
return <h1>Hello</h1>
<p>World</p>;
```

Correct JSX:

```
jsx
```

```
return (
  <div>
```

```
    <h1>Hello</h1>
    <p>World</p>
  </div>
);
```

- **Self-Closing Tags**: Just like in XML, JSX requires that tags with no content, like `<img>` or `<input>`, be self-closing.

  Correct JSX:

  jsx

```
<img src="image.jpg" alt="A picture" />
```

- **Expressions Inside JSX**: You can use **JavaScript expressions** inside JSX by wrapping them in curly braces {}. This allows you to dynamically insert values, variables, and expressions directly into the markup.

  Example:

  jsx

```
const name = "John";
return <h1>Hello, {name}!</h1>;
```

46

- **Event Handling in JSX**: Event names in JSX are written in camelCase (e.g., onClick, onChange), unlike the lowercase names in HTML.

Example:

jsx

```
<button        onClick={handleClick}>Click
Me</button>
```

4.3 Understanding Expressions Inside JSX

In JSX, you can embed any **JavaScript expression** inside curly braces {}. Expressions can be variables, function calls, mathematical operations, and more. This feature makes JSX powerful and allows you to dynamically generate content based on the state or props of your components.

Some examples of valid JavaScript expressions that you can use in JSX include:

1. **Variables**: You can embed a variable's value inside JSX.

   jsx

   ```
   const name = "Alice";
   ```

```
return <h1>Hello, {name}!</h1>;
```

2. **Mathematical Operations**: You can use mathematical expressions directly inside JSX.

```jsx
const a = 5;
const b = 10;
return <h1>{a + b}</h1>; // Outputs: 15
```

3. **Conditional Expressions**: JSX supports **ternary operators** for conditional rendering.

```jsx
const isLoggedIn = true;
return <h1>{isLoggedIn ? "Welcome, User!" : "Please Log In"}</h1>;
```

4. **Function Calls**: You can call functions or methods inside JSX expressions.

```jsx
function greet() {
    return "Hello, World!";
}
return <h1>{greet()}</h1>;
```

5. **Objects and Arrays**: You can use arrays and objects in JSX, although arrays need to be rendered into valid JSX elements (e.g., with .map()).

jsx

```
const    fruits   =    ["Apple",    "Banana",
"Orange"];
return (
  <ul>
    {fruits.map(fruit         =>         <li
key={fruit}>{fruit}</li>)}
  </ul>
);
```

Explanation:

- The fruits array is mapped to a list of <li> elements.
- Each <li> element is given a unique key prop to help React optimize rendering.

4.4 Real-World Example: Converting a Simple HTML Page into JSX

Now, let's convert a simple **HTML page** into **JSX** and see how it can be used within a React component.

Simple HTML Page:

html

```
<!DOCTYPE html>
<html lang="en">
<head>
  <meta charset="UTF-8">
  <title>Simple Page</title>
</head>
<body>
  <h1>Welcome to My Webpage</h1>
  <p>This is a simple webpage.</p>
  <button                 onclick="alert('Button
clicked!')">Click Me</button>
</body>
</html>
```

Now, let's convert this into a **React component** using JSX:

Converted JSX Code:

jsx

```
import React from 'react';

function SimplePage() {
  const handleClick = () => {
    alert("Button clicked!");
  };
```

```
  return (
    <div>
      <h1>Welcome to My Webpage</h1>
      <p>This is a simple webpage.</p>
      <button        onClick={handleClick}>Click
Me</button>
    </div>
  );
}
```

```
export default SimplePage;
```

Explanation:

- The h1 and p elements are identical in JSX, but we now have a **React component** that renders these elements.

- The onclick event is replaced with onClick in JSX, and the event handler (handleClick) is defined as a JavaScript function inside the component.

- The div element wraps everything because JSX requires a single root element.

In this chapter, we explored **JSX**, the syntax extension for JavaScript that allows you to write HTML-like code inside your React components. We discussed how JSX looks similar to HTML but has some important differences, such as the use of `className` instead of `class` and the requirement for self-closing tags. We also saw how to use **JavaScript expressions** within JSX to dynamically render content, including variables, conditionals, and function calls.

Finally, we walked through a real-world example of converting a simple HTML page into JSX within a React component. With this foundational understanding of JSX, you're now ready to build dynamic UIs with React in an efficient and readable manner.

In the next chapter, we will explore **React Components** in more detail, including how to pass data between components using **props**, manage internal state, and handle user interactions. Let's continue building!

CHAPTER 5

PROPS – PASSING DATA BETWEEN COMPONENTS

In this chapter, we will dive into **props**, one of the most important concepts in React. **Props** (short for "properties") are how data is passed between React components. They allow components to communicate with each other and make your components customizable. Understanding how to use props effectively is key to building dynamic and interactive React applications.

We will also explore **real-world examples** to solidify your understanding of how props work in practice.

5.1 What Are Props and How They Allow Components to Communicate?

In React, components are the building blocks of your application. Each component can manage its own state, but often you need to pass information between components. This is where **props** come in.

Props are how data is passed from one component to another, specifically from a **parent component** to a **child component**. They allow you to customize components and make them more flexible. Props are **read-only** and should not be modified by the child components—they can only be accessed and used to render the UI or trigger actions.

How props work:

- A parent component passes props to a child component.
- The child component can then access and display the values passed via props.
- Props make components reusable, as you can pass different values to the same component at different times.

5.2 Using Props to Customize Components

Props allow you to customize the behavior and appearance of a component by passing data to it. This means you can create a single component and reuse it with different values based on the data passed through props.

Basic Syntax for Using Props:

1. **Passing props from parent to child**: When rendering a child component, the parent component passes data via props.

jsx

```jsx
// Parent Component
function ParentComponent() {
  return <ChildComponent name="Alice" age={25} />;
}
```

2. **Accessing props inside the child component**: Inside the child component, you access the passed props using props.

jsx

```jsx
// Child Component
function ChildComponent(props) {
  return (
    <div>
      <h1>Hello, my name is {props.name}</h1>
      <p>I am {props.age} years old.</p>
    </div>
  );
}
```

In this example:

- The `ParentComponent` passes the `name` and `age` props to the `ChildComponent`.
- The `ChildComponent` then uses these props to render the name and age.

Key points to remember:

- Props are passed **downwards** from parent to child, meaning that a parent component has control over the data it sends to the child.
- Props can contain any kind of data: strings, numbers, arrays, functions, objects, and even other React components.

5.3 Real-World Example: Building a "Greeting" Component That Accepts Props

---

Let's put props into practice by building a simple **Greeting** component that accepts a user's name as a prop and displays a customized greeting message.

Step 1: Create the Greeting Component

First, let's create a `Greeting` component that accepts a `name` prop and renders a greeting message.

jsx

```
import React from 'react';

// Greeting Component
function Greeting(props) {
  return <h1>Hello, {props.name}!</h1>;
}

export default Greeting;
```

Explanation:

- The `Greeting` component accepts a `name` prop and renders a personalized greeting message by accessing `props.name`.

Step 2: Use the Greeting Component in a Parent Component

Now, let's create a parent component that uses the `Greeting` component and passes a name to it.

jsx

```
import React from 'react';
import Greeting from './Greeting';

// Parent Component
function App() {
  return (
    <div>
      <Greeting name="John" />
      <Greeting name="Alice" />
      <Greeting name="Bob" />
    </div>
  );
}

export default App;
```

Explanation:

- The App component acts as the parent, rendering multiple Greeting components.
- The name prop is passed different values ("John", "Alice", and "Bob") to the Greeting component each time, customizing the greeting for each one.

Step 3: Running the App

When you run the app, you'll see the following output:

58

```
Hello, John!
Hello, Alice!
Hello, Bob!
```

Each instance of the `Greeting` component displays a personalized message based on the `name` prop passed from the parent.

5.4 Props and Dynamic Content

One of the key benefits of using props is that they allow components to be **dynamic**. This means that you can reuse a single component and change its behavior based on the props passed to it.

For example, let's build a `ProfileCard` component that accepts props for a user's name, age, and bio. This component can be used for multiple users, each with different information.

Step 1: Create the ProfileCard Component

```jsx
import React from 'react';

function ProfileCard(props) {
  return (
```

```jsx
    <div className="profile-card">
      <h2>{props.name}</h2>
      <p>Age: {props.age}</p>
      <p>{props.bio}</p>
    </div>
  );
}


export default ProfileCard;
```

Step 2: Use the ProfileCard Component

Now, let's use the `ProfileCard` component in a parent component and pass different data via props for multiple users.

jsx

```jsx
import React from 'react';
import ProfileCard from './ProfileCard';

function App() {
  return (
    <div>
      <ProfileCard   name="John   Doe"   age={28}
bio="A software developer from NYC." />
      <ProfileCard   name="Jane   Smith"   age={32}
bio="A passionate graphic designer." />
    </div>
  );
}
```

```
export default App;
```

Explanation:

- Each `ProfileCard` is customized with different values for `name`, `age`, and `bio` props.
- The `ProfileCard` component is reused, but the information displayed inside the card changes based on the props passed to it.

5.5 Default Props and Prop Types

While props allow for flexible and customizable components, it's important to ensure that the props being passed into a component are of the correct type and have the expected values. React provides two tools for managing props:

1. **Default Props**: You can set default values for props in case the parent doesn't pass a value.

   Example:

   ```jsx
   jsx

   function Greeting(props) {
     return <h1>Hello, {props.name}!</h1>;
   ```

61

```
}
```

```
Greeting.defaultProps = {
  name: 'Guest',
};
```

If no `name` prop is provided, the component will default to "Guest".

2. **Prop Types**: You can use `PropTypes` to enforce that the props passed into a component are of the correct type. This helps catch bugs during development.

   Example:

   ```jsx
   import PropTypes from 'prop-types';

   function Greeting(props) {
     return <h1>Hello, {props.name}!</h1>;
   }

   Greeting.propTypes = {
     name: PropTypes.string.isRequired,
   };
   ```

   This ensures that the `name` prop is always a string and is required when using the `Greeting` component.

Conclusion

In this chapter, we learned about **props** in React and how they allow different components to communicate with each other. Props enable the customization of components and make them reusable, allowing the same component to be rendered with different data.

Key concepts covered:

- Props are used to pass data from parent components to child components.
- Props are **read-only** and should not be modified by child components.
- We explored real-world examples, such as creating a **Greeting** component that accepts props.
- We learned how to use **default props** and **prop types** to manage props effectively.

In the next chapter, we will dive into **state** and learn how it differs from props, how to use it to make components interactive, and how state can be managed in both class and functional components. Let's continue building our React skills!

CHAPTER 6

STATE – MAKING COMPONENTS INTERACTIVE

In this chapter, we will explore **state**, one of the most essential concepts in React. While **props** are used to pass data between components, **state** is used to manage data within a component that can change over time, especially as a result of user interaction. State allows components to become **interactive** and **dynamic**. Understanding how to manage and update state in React will make your components much more powerful and responsive.

We will cover:

- What state is and how it makes components interactive.
- How to manage state in **class components** and **functional components**.
- A **real-world example** of building a simple counter application to demonstrate how state is used.

6.1 What is State and How It's Used to Make React Components Interactive?

In React, **state** refers to a JavaScript object that holds data that can change over time. This data is specific to a component and can be updated based on user interaction, API responses, or any other events in the application.

- **State in React** is typically used for data that **changes** during the lifecycle of a component. This could be something like:
    - User input (e.g., a form field or a button click).
    - A value that updates over time (e.g., a timer or a counter).
    - Data fetched from an API.
- When the state of a component changes, React **re-renders** that component to reflect the new data, ensuring the UI stays in sync with the state.

For example, when you click a button to increase a counter, the counter value changes, and React automatically updates the UI to reflect this change.

6.2 Managing State in Class Components vs. Functional Components

React provides two ways to manage state: in **class components** and in **functional components**.

Managing State in Class Components

In **class components**, state is managed using the `this.state` object. You can initialize the state in the constructor and update it with `this.setState()`. When you call `this.setState()`, React triggers a re-render of the component to reflect the updated state.

Example: Managing state in a class component.

```jsx
import React, { Component } from 'react';

class Counter extends Component {
  constructor(props) {
    super(props);
    this.state = {
      count: 0
    };
  }

  increment = () => {
    this.setState({ count: this.state.count + 1
});
  };

  render() {
    return (
```

66

```
<div>
  <p>Count: {this.state.count}</p>
  <button
onClick={this.increment}>Increment</button>
  </div>
  );
  }
}


export default Counter;
```

Explanation:

- The `Counter` component is a class component that initializes its state with a `count` property set to `0`.
- The `increment` method updates the `count` state by calling `this.setState()`, which triggers a re-render of the component.
- When the button is clicked, the count increases by 1, and the updated value is displayed in the UI.

Managing State in Functional Components

In **functional components**, state is managed using the **`useState` hook** (introduced in React 16.8). The `useState` hook allows you to add state to functional components, making them as powerful as class components in terms of interactivity.

Example: Managing state in a functional component.

jsx

```
import React, { useState } from 'react';

function Counter() {
  const [count, setCount] = useState(0); // count
is the state variable, setCount is the function
to update the state

  const increment = () => {
    setCount(count + 1); // Update the count
state
  };

  return (
    <div>
      <p>Count: {count}</p>
      <button
onClick={increment}>Increment</button>
    </div>
  );
}

export default Counter;
```

Explanation:

- The `useState` hook is used to declare the state variable `count` and the function `setCount` to update the state.
- The `increment` function updates the state by calling `setCount(count + 1)`.
- Like in the class component, clicking the button increases the count by 1, and the component re-renders to display the updated count.

When to use each?

- **Class components**: Use class components when you need to work with lifecycle methods, such as `componentDidMount` or `componentDidUpdate`. They are still commonly used, but with the introduction of hooks, functional components have become the preferred choice for most new code.
- **Functional components**: With the **useState** hook and other hooks like **useEffect**, **functional components** are now the recommended way to work with state and side effects in React. They are simpler and easier to work with, and most developers prefer them for new applications.

6.3 Real-World Example: Building a Counter Application Using State

To illustrate how state works in React, let's build a simple **counter application** that allows the user to increment a counter by clicking a button.

Step 1: Counter Component in a Functional Component

We'll use **useState** in a functional component to manage the state of the counter.

jsx

```
import React, { useState } from 'react';

function Counter() {
  // Declaring state variable `count` and
function `setCount` to update it
  const [count, setCount] = useState(0);

  // Function to increment the counter
  const increment = () => {
    setCount(count + 1); // Increment count by 1
  };

  // Function to reset the counter to 0
  const reset = () => {
    setCount(0); // Reset count to 0
  };

  return (
```

70

```
<div>
  <h1>Counter: {count}</h1>
  <button
onClick={increment}>Increment</button>
  <button onClick={reset}>Reset</button>
</div>
);
}

export default Counter;
```

Explanation:

- We define a state variable `count` with an initial value of `0` using the `useState` hook.
- The `increment` function updates the state by increasing the `count` by 1 every time the "Increment" button is clicked.
- We also have a `reset` function that sets the `count` back to `0` when the "Reset" button is clicked.
- The component re-renders automatically every time the state changes, ensuring that the updated `count` is displayed in the UI.

Step 2: Using the Counter Component in the Parent Component

Now, let's use the `Counter` component in a parent component.

jsx

```
import React from 'react';
import Counter from './Counter';

function App() {
  return (
    <div>
      <h1>React Counter App</h1>
      <Counter />
    </div>
  );
}

export default App;
```

6.4 Summary of Key Concepts

- **State** is a way for React components to manage their own data. It makes components interactive by allowing them to update and re-render in response to changes.
- **Class components** use `this.state` and `this.setState()` to manage state, while **functional components** use the `useState` hook.
- State can be used to update the UI dynamically based on user interaction (such as clicking a button or entering data into a form).

- In the **counter application**, we used state to track the `count` and updated it with button clicks.

6.5 Conclusion

In this chapter, we learned how **state** is used to make React components interactive and dynamic. We explored how to manage state in both **class components** and **functional components**, using `this.state` and the `useState` hook, respectively.

By building a simple **counter app**, we saw how state allows us to update the UI in response to user actions. Mastering state management is crucial to creating interactive React applications, and as you continue learning React, you'll see how state plays a central role in building sophisticated applications.

In the next chapter, we will dive into **event handling** in React and explore how to handle user inputs and interactions to build more complex applications. Let's continue building!

CHAPTER 7

EVENT HANDLING IN REACT

Handling user events is one of the core features of React. In this chapter, we will explore how to handle various user interactions such as clicks, form submissions, and key presses. We'll learn how to bind event handlers in both **class components** and **functional components** and look at the best practices for handling events in React.

By the end of this chapter, you'll have a clear understanding of how to interact with the user in your React apps. We'll also work through a real-world example: building a **to-do list** app that handles task addition.

7.1 Handling User Events in React

In React, **events** are handled through **event handlers**. Event handlers are functions that are executed when a specific event, such as a click or a form submission, occurs. React provides a set of synthetic events that wrap around the browser's native events, ensuring that events work consistently across different browsers.

Common user events in React include:

- **Click Events**: For buttons, links, etc.
- **Form Submission**: For handling form data.
- **Keyboard Events**: For key presses, like "Enter" or "Escape".

React uses a declarative approach to handle events, meaning you define the event handler function in the component, and React automatically binds it to the DOM element when it renders.

7.2 Binding Event Handlers in Class Components

In **class components**, event handlers need to be bound to the component's instance. This ensures that the `this` keyword inside the event handler refers to the component instance, allowing you to access the component's state and other methods.

In React, binding an event handler in a class component can be done in two ways:

1. **Binding in the constructor** (traditional method).
2. **Using arrow functions** (more modern approach).

1. Binding in the Constructor

In this approach, the event handler method is bound to the component instance inside the constructor.

Example:

jsx

```
import React, { Component } from 'react';

class Counter extends Component {
  constructor(props) {
    super(props);
    this.state = { count: 0 };
    this.increment = this.increment.bind(this);
// Binding the method here
  }

  increment() {
    this.setState({ count: this.state.count + 1
});
  }

  render() {
    return (
      <div>
        <h1>Count: {this.state.count}</h1>
```

```
      <button
onClick={this.increment}>Increment</button>
      </div>
    );
  }
}


export default Counter;
```

Explanation:

- In the `constructor`, the `increment` method is explicitly bound to `this` using `.bind(this)`.
- When you click the "Increment" button, the `increment` function is called, and the state is updated.

2. Using Arrow Functions (More Modern Approach)

You can use arrow functions to automatically bind the event handler to the component instance. This is a cleaner approach, especially in smaller components.

Example:

```
jsx

import React, { Component } from 'react';

class Counter extends Component {
```

```
  state = { count: 0 };

  increment  =  ()  =>  {    // Arrow function
automatically binds `this`
    this.setState({ count: this.state.count + 1
});
  };

  render() {
    return (
      <div>
        <h1>Count: {this.state.count}</h1>
        <button
onClick={this.increment}>Increment</button>
      </div>
    );
  }
}

export default Counter;
```

Explanation:

- The increment method is written as an **arrow function**.
- Arrow functions automatically bind this to the current instance of the class, so you don't need to explicitly bind it in the constructor.

7.3 Event Handling in Functional Components

In **functional components**, event handling is straightforward and doesn't require binding methods like in class components. Event handlers are simply functions defined within the component, and you can directly pass them as props to the event.

Example:

```jsx
import React, { useState } from 'react';

function Counter() {
  const [count, setCount] = useState(0);

  const increment = () => {
    setCount(count + 1);
  };

  return (
    <div>
      <h1>Count: {count}</h1>
      <button
onClick={increment}>Increment</button>
    </div>
  );
}
```

```
export default Counter;
```

Explanation:

- We use the `useState` hook to manage the `count` state.
- The `increment` function is defined inside the component and passed directly to the `onClick` event handler.
- There's no need to bind `this` as there is no class instance in functional components.

7.4 Real-World Example: Creating a To-Do List App That Handles Task Addition

---

Let's now build a **to-do list** app where the user can add tasks. We will use event handling to capture user input and update the state.

Step 1: Create the To-Do List Component

We will create a functional component that lets users add tasks to a list by entering text into a form and clicking a button.

jsx

```
import React, { useState } from 'react';
```

```
function TodoApp() {
  const [task, setTask] = useState('');         //
To store the current task
  const [tasks, setTasks] = useState([]);        //
To store all tasks in the list

  // Handle task input change
  const handleChange = (event) => {
    setTask(event.target.value);  // Update task
state as user types
  };

  // Handle form submission to add task
  const handleSubmit = (event) => {
    event.preventDefault();      // Prevent  page
refresh on form submission
    if (task.trim()) {
      setTasks([...tasks, task]);   // Add  new
task to the list
      setTask('');  // Clear the input field
    }
  };

  return (
    <div>
      <h1>To-Do List</h1>
      <form onSubmit={handleSubmit}>
        <input
          type="text"
```

81

```
            value={task}
            onChange={handleChange}
            placeholder="Enter task"
          />
          <button type="submit">Add Task</button>
        </form>
        <ul>
          {tasks.map((task, index) => (
            <li key={index}>{task}</li>  // Render
tasks in a list
          ))}
        </ul>
      </div>
    );
}

export default TodoApp;
```

Explanation:

- **State Variables**: We have two state variables:
    - task for holding the current input value.
    - tasks for storing the list of all tasks.
- **handleChange**: This function updates the task state every time the user types in the input field.
- **handleSubmit**: This function adds the current task to the list when the user submits the form. It also prevents the default form behavior, clears the input field, and updates the tasks state.

- **Rendering the Task List**: The tasks are displayed in an unordered list (`<ul>`) using the `map()` function.

Step 2: Using the To-Do List Component in the Parent Component

Let's render the `TodoApp` component inside a parent component:

jsx

```
import React from 'react';
import TodoApp from './TodoApp';

function App() {
  return (
    <div>
      <h1>My To-Do App</h1>
      <TodoApp />
    </div>
  );
}

export default App;
```

7.5 Summary of Key Concepts

- **Event Handling**: React uses event handlers to manage user interactions like clicks, form submissions, and key presses.

- **Binding Methods in Class Components**: In class components, you need to bind event handlers to the component's instance using `.bind()` or arrow functions.

- **Event Handling in Functional Components**: Functional components use functions directly as event handlers, and there's no need for binding as `this` is not used.

- **Form Handling**: React allows you to handle user input efficiently with forms, capturing input values, and updating the state.

7.6 Conclusion

In this chapter, we learned how to handle user events in React, making components interactive and responsive to user input. We covered binding event handlers in **class components**, passing event handlers in **functional components**, and handling common events such as **clicks** and **form submissions**.

We also built a **to-do list app** as a real-world example, where users can add tasks by typing in an input field and clicking a button. This app demonstrated how React's event handling and state management work together to update the UI dynamically.

In the next chapter, we will explore **conditional rendering** in React, which allows you to render different components or elements based on certain conditions, making your applications more flexible and dynamic. Let's continue building!

CHAPTER 8

CONDITIONAL RENDERING IN REACT

In this chapter, we will explore **conditional rendering** in React. Conditional rendering allows you to display different UI elements or components based on specific conditions. This feature is essential for creating dynamic and interactive user interfaces, as it enables you to control what the user sees based on various states or conditions (e.g., user authentication, form validation, or network requests).

We will cover:

- How to render different UI elements based on conditions.
- Using **if statements**, **ternary operators**, and **logical &&
operators** for conditional rendering.
- A **real-world example** of displaying different content based on user authentication.

8.1 How to Render Different UI Elements Based on Conditions

In React, **conditional rendering** means you decide which elements to render based on the current state, props, or other conditions. React will **render** only the components or elements that are relevant for the current condition.

You can apply conditional rendering using:

- **If-else statements** for more complex conditions.
- **Ternary operators** for concise inline conditions.
- **Logical AND (&&) operators** for simpler conditions.

React doesn't directly use HTML `if` statements for rendering. Instead, you use JavaScript expressions inside JSX to conditionally decide what should be rendered.

8.2 Using if Statements, Ternary Operators, and Logical && Operators for Conditional Rendering

1. Using if Statements for Conditional Rendering

The `if` **statement** is commonly used for more complex conditions. You can define the condition outside of the JSX code, and then return the appropriate JSX based on that condition.

Example:

```jsx
function WelcomeMessage({ isLoggedIn }) {
  if (isLoggedIn) {
    return <h1>Welcome back, User!</h1>;
  } else {
    return <h1>Please log in</h1>;
  }
}
```

Explanation:

- The `if` statement checks whether the `isLoggedIn` prop is `true` or `false`.
- If the user is logged in, it renders a personalized message. If not, it prompts the user to log in.

2. Using Ternary Operator for Conditional Rendering

The **ternary operator** is a shorthand version of an `if-else` statement. It's ideal for concise conditional rendering in JSX.

Syntax:

```jsx
condition ? expressionIfTrue : expressionIfFalse
```

Example:

```jsx

function Greeting({ isLoggedIn }) {
  return (
    <h1>{isLoggedIn ? "Welcome back, User!" :
"Please log in"}</h1>
  );
}
```

Explanation:

- The ternary operator checks if `isLoggedIn` is `true` or `false` and renders the corresponding message.
- This is a compact and readable way of writing conditional rendering directly inside JSX.

3. Using Logical AND (`&&`) Operator for Conditional Rendering

The **logical `&&` operator** can also be used to conditionally render elements. This approach is often used when you only want to render something if a condition is `true`, and nothing otherwise.

Syntax:

```jsx

condition && expression
```

Example:

```jsx

function UserProfile({ user }) {
  return (
    <div>
      <h1>User Profile</h1>
      {user && <p>Welcome, {user.name}!</p>} {/*
Only render if `user` exists */}
    </div>
  );
}
```

Explanation:

- The `&&` operator ensures that the `<p>` element is only rendered if the `user` object exists (i.e., `user` is not `null` or `undefined`).
- If `user` is `null`, nothing will be rendered after `&&`.

8.3 Real-World Example: Displaying Different Content Based on User Authentication

---

A common use case for conditional rendering is **user authentication**. Based on whether a user is logged in or not, we may want to display different UI elements, such as a login form or a welcome message.

Step 1: Create the Authentication Component

In this example, we will create a simple component that displays different content based on whether the user is logged in or not.

```jsx
import React, { useState } from 'react';

function AuthApp() {
  const [isLoggedIn, setIsLoggedIn] = useState(false);

  const handleLogin = () => {
    setIsLoggedIn(true);    // Simulate a successful login
  };

  const handleLogout = () => {
    setIsLoggedIn(false); // Simulate logout
  };

  return (
    <div>
      <h1>Authentication Example</h1>
      {isLoggedIn ? (
        <div>
          <h2>Welcome back, User!</h2>
```

```
        <button      onClick={handleLogout}>Log
out</button>
      </div>
    ) : (
      <div>
        <h2>Please log in to continue.</h2>
        <button      onClick={handleLogin}>Log
in</button>
      </div>
    )}
  </div>
);
}
```

```
export default AuthApp;
```

Explanation:

- We use the useState hook to manage the isLoggedIn state.
- When the user clicks the "Log in" button, the handleLogin function sets isLoggedIn to true.
- When the user clicks the "Log out" button, the handleLogout function sets isLoggedIn back to false.
- Using the **ternary operator**, we conditionally render either the "Welcome" message and "Log out" button or

the "Please log in" message and "Log in" button, depending on the `isLoggedIn` state.

Step 2: Using the AuthApp Component in the Main App

Now, let's render the `AuthApp` component inside the main `App` component.

jsx

```
import React from 'react';
import AuthApp from './AuthApp';

function App() {
  return (
    <div>
      <h1>My React App</h1>
      <AuthApp />
    </div>
  );
}

export default App;
```

8.4 Summary of Key Concepts

- **Conditional Rendering**: React allows you to conditionally render different elements based on certain conditions, making your components dynamic and interactive.
- **if Statements**: The `if` statement can be used outside JSX to control the rendering of components based on conditions.
- **Ternary Operators**: The ternary operator provides a concise way to render content conditionally directly within JSX.
- **Logical && Operators**: The logical `&&` operator is a simple way to render elements only when a condition is true, without having to write an `else` case.

8.5 Conclusion

In this chapter, we learned about **conditional rendering** in React and how to display different content based on conditions. Whether using **if statements**, **ternary operators**, or **logical &&**, React provides flexible tools for controlling the UI dynamically. We also worked through a real-world example of **user authentication**, where we conditionally displayed either a "log in" or "log out" button based on the authentication state.

Mastering conditional rendering is an essential skill for creating interactive and responsive React applications. In the next chapter, we will explore **lists and keys in React**, another crucial concept for rendering dynamic content efficiently. Let's continue building!

CHAPTER 9

LISTS AND KEYS IN REACT

In this chapter, we will learn how to render **lists of elements** in React, which is a common task when working with dynamic data. Rendering lists in React is straightforward with the map() function, but there are important considerations, particularly around **keys**, that can significantly impact performance. We will explore how to efficiently render lists and ensure optimal performance by understanding the role of keys in list rendering.

By the end of this chapter, you'll understand how to handle lists in React and avoid performance issues while working with dynamic content.

9.1 Rendering Lists of Elements Using the map() Function

React makes it easy to render **lists of elements** dynamically using the **map()** function. The map() function is a standard JavaScript method that iterates over an array and applies a function to each item, returning a new array. In React, you can use map() to loop over an array and return JSX elements.

The general syntax for rendering a list in React looks like this:

```jsx
const items = ['Apple', 'Banana', 'Orange'];

const listItems = items.map((item, index) => (
  <li key={index}>{item}</li>
));
```

In this example:

- **map()** is used to iterate over the items array.
- Each item in the array is rendered as an `<li>` element.
- The **key** prop is necessary to help React optimize the rendering process (discussed later).

Rendering the List in JSX:

```jsx
function FruitList() {
  const fruits = ['Apple', 'Banana', 'Orange'];

  return (
    <ul>
      {fruits.map((fruit, index) => (
        <li key={index}>{fruit}</li>
      ))}
```

```
    </ul>
  );
}
```

Explanation:

- The `fruits` array is mapped to a list of `<li>` elements inside a `<ul>`.
- Each list item is assigned a unique **key** to help React identify and track elements efficiently during re-renders.

9.2 The Importance of Keys in List Rendering for Optimal Performance

---

In React, when rendering a list of elements, it is important to provide a **unique key prop** to each element in the list. **Keys** help React identify which items have changed, been added, or removed, thus optimizing the process of updating the DOM.

Without keys, React would have to re-render the entire list of items every time a change occurs, leading to unnecessary performance overhead. By using keys, React can efficiently update only the items that have changed, minimizing the number of re-renders and improving performance.

Why Are Keys Important?

- **Optimized Re-renders**: When you update the list (e.g., adding or removing an item), React uses the key to match the previous list of elements with the new list, efficiently determining which elements need to be updated.
- **Tracking Items**: React uses the `key` prop to track each element in the list. This allows React to maintain the correct order of items and preserve their state (e.g., form values, animation states).

How to Choose Keys

- **Use unique, stable values**: The best practice is to use **unique IDs** or other stable values (e.g., database IDs) as keys. Avoid using indexes as keys, especially if the list can change dynamically (items may be added, removed, or reordered).

Using array indices as keys is not recommended if the order of elements might change, as it can lead to issues with component state and performance:

```jsx
// Avoid using index as the key if the list
changes dynamically
{fruits.map((fruit, index) => (
```

```
    <li key={index}>{fruit}</li>
))}
```

Instead, use a stable, unique identifier, like an id:

jsx

```
const fruits = [
    { id: 1, name: 'Apple' },
    { id: 2, name: 'Banana' },
    { id: 3, name: 'Orange' },
];

{fruits.map(fruit => (
    <li key={fruit.id}>{fruit.name}</li>
))}
```

Explanation:

- Here, the key is set to fruit.id, which is unique for each item in the list.
- By using stable IDs as keys, React can correctly identify and update the items in the list.

9.3 Real-World Example: Displaying a List of Items Like a Shopping Cart

---

Let's implement a **shopping cart** where users can add and remove items. This example will demonstrate how to manage a list of items in React using state, handle dynamic updates, and efficiently render the list with keys.

Step 1: Create the ShoppingCart Component

jsx

```
import React, { useState } from 'react';

function ShoppingCart() {
  const [cartItems, setCartItems] = useState([
    { id: 1, name: 'Apple', price: 1.5 },
    { id: 2, name: 'Banana', price: 1.2 },
    { id: 3, name: 'Orange', price: 1.8 }
  ]);

  // Function to remove an item from the cart
  const removeItem = (id) => {
    setCartItems(cartItems.filter(item         =>
item.id !== id));
  };

  return (
    <div>
      <h2>Shopping Cart</h2>
      <ul>
        {cartItems.map(item => (
          <li key={item.id}>
```

```
        {item.name} - ${item.price}
        <button          onClick={()          =>
removeItem(item.id)}>Remove</button>
      </li>
    ))}
  </ul>
  <p>Total: ${cartItems.reduce((total, item)
=> total + item.price, 0).toFixed(2)}</p>
  </div>
  );
}


export default ShoppingCart;
```

Explanation:

- **State Management**: We initialize the `cartItems` state with an array of items, where each item has an `id`, `name`, and `price`.

- **removeItem Function**: The `removeItem` function removes an item from the cart by filtering out the item with the specified `id`.

- **Rendering the List**: We use `map()` to iterate over `cartItems` and render each item in an unordered list. Each list item is assigned a `key` based on the unique `id` of the item.

- **Calculating the Total**: The total price is calculated using the `reduce()` function, which sums up the prices of all items in the cart.

Step 2: Using the ShoppingCart Component

Now, let's render the `ShoppingCart` component in the main `App` component.

jsx

```jsx
import React from 'react';
import ShoppingCart from './ShoppingCart';

function App() {
  return (
    <div>
      <h1>My React Shopping Cart</h1>
      <ShoppingCart />
    </div>
  );
}

export default App;
```

9.4 Summary of Key Concepts

- **Rendering Lists in React**: Use the `map()` function to loop through arrays and render list items as JSX elements.

- **Importance of Keys**: The `key` prop is critical when rendering lists in React. It helps React efficiently update the DOM when items are added, removed, or reordered.

- **Choosing Stable Keys**: Use unique and stable values (e.g., IDs) as keys rather than array indices to avoid potential issues when the list changes.

- **Real-World Example**: We created a shopping cart where items can be added and removed dynamically. We used the `map()` function to render the cart items and `key` to optimize rendering.

9.5 Conclusion

In this chapter, we explored **lists and keys** in React, which are fundamental concepts for rendering dynamic content. We learned how to use the `map()` function to iterate over an array of items and render them in JSX. We also discussed the importance of the `key` prop for performance optimization, ensuring that React can efficiently update the DOM.

We then applied these concepts in a real-world example, creating a shopping cart that dynamically updates as items are added or removed. Understanding how to manage and render lists effectively will allow you to build more interactive and complex applications.

In the next chapter, we will dive into **forms in React**, exploring how to handle user input and perform validation. Let's keep building!

CHAPTER 10

FORMS IN REACT

Forms are one of the most common ways to collect user input in web applications. In React, handling forms involves more than just rendering form elements. We need to manage form data, handle user input, and validate the data before submission. React provides a powerful way to manage form inputs using **controlled components**.

In this chapter, we'll dive into the following:

- How to handle form data with **controlled components**.
- Managing form inputs and validation to ensure the data is correct before submission.
- A **real-world example** of creating a simple form to collect user information.

10.1 Handling Form Data with Controlled Components

In React, a **controlled component** is an input element whose value is controlled by the **React state**. This means the state serves as the "single source of truth" for the form data. React makes it easy to handle form data by linking input elements with the component's state, allowing us to manage user input dynamically.

Controlled Components:

- The value of an input field is controlled by the state of the component.
- Every change to the input field updates the state using an event handler, typically the onChange event.
- The form data is synchronized with React's state, which ensures that React manages and controls the form input values.

Example of a controlled input in a form:

```jsx
import React, { useState } from 'react';

function Form() {
  const [name, setName] = useState('');

  // Handle changes to the input field
  const handleChange = (event) => {
    setName(event.target.value); // Update the
state with input value
  };

  const handleSubmit = (event) => {
```

107

```
    event.preventDefault();    // Prevent page
reload on form submission
    alert('Submitted: ' + name);
  };


  return (
    <form onSubmit={handleSubmit}>
      <label>
        Name:
        <input      type="text"      value={name}
onChange={handleChange} />
      </label>
      <button type="submit">Submit</button>
    </form>
  );
}


export default Form;
```

Explanation:

- The `input` element's `value` is tied to the `name` state, making it a controlled component.
- The `onChange` event is used to update the `name` state whenever the user types in the input field.
- When the form is submitted, we use `event.preventDefault()` to prevent the page from reloading, and then display the value of `name` in an alert.

10.2 Managing Form Inputs and Validation

In real-world applications, you often need to handle multiple form fields and validate the data before submission. React makes it easy to manage complex forms by using **controlled components** for each input field. You can also apply **form validation** to ensure that the data meets the required format (e.g., email validation, required fields).

Managing Multiple Form Inputs

If your form has multiple input fields, you can manage each one using state. For more complex forms, you can group the form data into a single object and update individual fields as needed.

Example: Handling multiple inputs (name, email) in a form.

jsx

```
import React, { useState } from 'react';

function UserForm() {
  const [formData, setFormData] = useState({
    name: '',
    email: ''
  });
```

```
const handleChange = (event) => {
  const { name, value } = event.target;
  setFormData({
    ...formData,
    [name]: value
  });
};

const handleSubmit = (event) => {
  event.preventDefault();
  alert('Form        submitted:          '          +
JSON.stringify(formData));
};

return (
  <form onSubmit={handleSubmit}>
    <label>
      Name:
      <input
        type="text"
        name="name"
        value={formData.name}
        onChange={handleChange}
      />
    </label>
    <label>
      Email:
      <input
```

```
        type="email"
        name="email"
        value={formData.email}
        onChange={handleChange}
      />
    </label>
    <button type="submit">Submit</button>
  </form>
);
}

export default UserForm;
```

Explanation:

- The `formData` state object holds the values for both the `name` and `email` input fields.
- The `handleChange` function updates the corresponding value in the state based on the `name` attribute of the input.
- When the form is submitted, the `formData` object is displayed using `JSON.stringify()`.

Form Validation

In real-world applications, you often need to ensure that the form data is valid before allowing the user to submit the form. React allows you to implement simple validation logic directly in the event handlers.

Example: Adding basic form validation (required fields).

jsx

```
import React, { useState } from 'react';

function UserForm() {
  const [formData, setFormData] = useState({
    name: '',
    email: ''
  });
  const [error, setError] = useState('');

  const handleChange = (event) => {
    const { name, value } = event.target;
    setFormData({
      ...formData,
      [name]: value
    });
  };

  const validateForm = () => {
    if (!formData.name || !formData.email) {
      setError('Both fields are required.');
      return false;
    }
    setError('');
    return true;
  };
```

```
const handleSubmit = (event) => {
  event.preventDefault();
  if (validateForm()) {
    alert('Form      submitted:      '      +
JSON.stringify(formData));
  }
};


return (
  <form onSubmit={handleSubmit}>
    <label>
      Name:
      <input
        type="text"
        name="name"
        value={formData.name}
        onChange={handleChange}
      />
    </label>
    <label>
      Email:
      <input
        type="email"
        name="email"
        value={formData.email}
        onChange={handleChange}
      />
    </label>
```

```
    {error  &&  <p  style={{  color:  'red'
}}>{error}</p>}
      <button type="submit">Submit</button>
    </form>
  );
}


export default UserForm;
```

Explanation:

- We added a new state variable `error` to hold the validation error message.
- The `validateForm` function checks if both the `name` and `email` fields are filled out. If any field is empty, an error message is set, and the form is not submitted.
- If the form is valid, the form data is displayed upon submission.

10.3 Real-World Example: Creating a Simple Form to Collect User Information

---

Let's implement a **simple form** that collects a user's name, email, and age. This form will allow the user to submit the information after validating the inputs.

Step 1: Create the UserForm Component

jsx

```jsx
import React, { useState } from 'react';

function UserForm() {
  const [formData, setFormData] = useState({
    name: '',
    email: '',
    age: ''
  });
  const [error, setError] = useState('');

  const handleChange = (event) => {
    const { name, value } = event.target;
    setFormData({
      ...formData,
      [name]: value
    });
  };

  const validateForm = () => {
    if (!formData.name || !formData.email ||
!formData.age) {
      setError('All fields are required.');
      return false;
    }
    setError('');
    return true;
```

115

```
  };

  const handleSubmit = (event) => {
    event.preventDefault();
    if (validateForm()) {
      alert('Form      submitted:        '      +
JSON.stringify(formData));
    }
  };

  return (
    <form onSubmit={handleSubmit}>
      <label>
        Name:
        <input
          type="text"
          name="name"
          value={formData.name}
          onChange={handleChange}
        />
      </label>
      <label>
        Email:
        <input
          type="email"
          name="email"
          value={formData.email}
          onChange={handleChange}
        />
```

```
      </label>
      <label>
        Age:    ·
        <input
          type="number"
          name="age"
          value={formData.age}
          onChange={handleChange}
        />
      </label>
      {error  &&  <p  style={{  color:  'red'
}}>{error}</p>}
      <button type="submit">Submit</button>
    </form>
  );
}

export default UserForm;
```

Explanation:

- The UserForm component handles form inputs for name, email, and age using controlled components.
- The validateForm function checks that all fields are filled out before submission.
- If the form is valid, the form data is displayed in an alert message after submission.

117

Step 2: Using the UserForm Component in the Main App

jsx

```jsx
import React from 'react';
import UserForm from './UserForm';

function App() {
  return (
    <div>
      <h1>React Form Example</h1>
      <UserForm />
    </div>
  );
}

export default App;
```

10.4 Summary of Key Concepts

- **Controlled Components**: In React, form elements are typically controlled components, meaning their values are tied to React's state, and changes are managed via event handlers.
- **Form Validation**: You can easily implement form validation to ensure that users provide valid input before submitting the form.

- **Managing Multiple Inputs**: Use state objects to manage multiple form fields, making it easier to update and handle multiple pieces of data.
- **Error Handling**: React allows you to manage validation errors and provide feedback to users, improving the overall user experience.

10.5 Conclusion

In this chapter, we explored **handling forms in React** with controlled components. We discussed how to manage form data, validate inputs, and ensure the form data is correct before submission. We also built a simple form to collect user information, demonstrating how React makes it easy to work with forms and handle user input dynamically.

In the next chapter, we will explore **lifting state up** in React, where we will see how to share data between components by moving state to a common parent component. Let's continue building!

CHAPTER 11

THE POWER OF REACT HOOKS

React Hooks have revolutionized the way developers write **functional components**. Before hooks were introduced in React 16.8, class components were required for features like **state management** and **side effects**. With hooks, functional components can now use state and side effects, which allows developers to write cleaner, more concise code without sacrificing functionality.

In this chapter, we will explore:

- An **introduction to hooks** and how they simplify functional components.
- The **useState** and **useEffect** hooks, two of the most important hooks in React.
- A **real-world example**: Converting a class-based component into a functional component using hooks.

11.1 Introduction to Hooks and How They Revolutionize Functional Components

Before hooks, React developers had to use **class components** to manage local state or perform side effects, which meant more boilerplate code. React Hooks simplify this by allowing functional components to handle state and side effects without using classes. This has made functional components much more powerful and easier to use.

Here's a summary of the major benefits of hooks:

- **Simplicity**: Functional components are simpler and easier to read and maintain compared to class components.
- **No More `this`**: With hooks, you no longer need to use `this` to refer to component instances, which simplifies your code.
- **Reusable Logic**: Hooks allow you to extract logic into custom hooks, making your code more modular and reusable.

The **most commonly used hooks** in React are:

- **`useState`**: For managing state in functional components.
- **`useEffect`**: For handling side effects like fetching data, subscriptions, and manual DOM manipulations.
- **`useContext`**: For managing global state with context.
- **`useReducer`**: For more complex state logic.

In this chapter, we'll focus on **useState** and **useEffect**, which are the two hooks most commonly used in day-to-day React development.

11.2 The useState Hook

The useState hook allows you to add **state** to **functional components**. It returns an array with two elements:

- The **current state value**.
- A function to **update** the state.

Basic Usage of useState

jsx

```jsx
import React, { useState } from 'react';

function Counter() {
  // Declare state variable `count` with initial
value of 0
  const [count, setCount] = useState(0);

  const increment = () => {
    setCount(count + 1); // Update the state
  };

  return (
```

```
    <div>
      <p>Count: {count}</p>
      <button
onClick={increment}>Increment</button>
    </div>
  );
}

export default Counter;
```

Explanation:

- The useState hook is called with an initial value (0), and it returns an array.
  - count is the state variable.
  - setCount is the function used to update count.
- When the button is clicked, the increment function is triggered, which updates the count state and re-renders the component with the new value.

Multiple State Variables

You can use useState multiple times in the same component to manage different pieces of state.

```
jsx

import React, { useState } from 'react';
```

123

```
function Counter() {
  const [count, setCount] = useState(0);
  const [name, setName] = useState('');

  return (
    <div>
      <p>Count: {count}</p>
      <button onClick={() => setCount(count +
1)}>Increment</button>

      <p>Name: {name}</p>
      <input
        type="text"
        value={name}
        onChange={(e)                         =>
setName(e.target.value)}
      />
    </div>
  );
}


export default Counter;
```

Explanation:

- The component manages two pieces of state: count and
  name.
- The useState hook is used separately for each variable.

124

11.3 The useEffect Hook

The useEffect hook allows you to perform **side effects** in your functional components. Side effects include actions like fetching data, setting up subscriptions, or manually changing the DOM. Before hooks, these actions had to be done in lifecycle methods like componentDidMount and componentDidUpdate in class components.

Basic Usage of useEffect

jsx

```jsx
import React, { useState, useEffect } from 'react';

function Timer() {
  const [time, setTime] = useState(0);

  useEffect(() => {
    const interval = setInterval(() => {
      setTime(prevTime => prevTime + 1);
    }, 1000);

    // Cleanup function to clear the interval
when the component unmounts
    return () => clearInterval(interval);
```

```
    }, []);  // The empty array means this effect
runs only once when the component mounts

    return <h1>{time} seconds</h1>;
}

export default Timer;
```

Explanation:

- `useEffect` is used to set up a timer that increments the `time` state every second.
- The effect function is run when the component mounts (because of the empty dependency array `[]`).
- **Cleanup**: The return function inside `useEffect` is used to **clean up** the side effect when the component unmounts. In this case, we clear the interval to prevent memory leaks.

Using `useEffect` with Dependencies

You can specify dependencies for the `useEffect` hook. The effect will run only when one of the dependencies changes.

```
jsx

import React, { useState, useEffect } from
'react';
```

```
function UserProfile({ userId }) {
  const [user, setUser] = useState(null);

  useEffect(() => {
    // Fetch user data whenever the userId
changes
    fetch(`/api/user/${userId}`)
      .then((response) => response.json())
      .then((data) => setUser(data));
  }, [userId]);   // Effect runs when `userId`
changes

  if (!user) return <div>Loading...</div>;

  return <div>User: {user.name}</div>;
}

export default UserProfile;
```

Explanation:

- The useEffect hook is set to run whenever the userId prop changes. This allows you to fetch new user data when the userId changes.
- The second argument to useEffect is an array of dependencies. React will re-run the effect when any of these dependencies change.

11.4 Real-World Example: Converting a Class-Based Component into a Functional One Using Hooks

Let's take a **class-based component** and convert it into a **functional component** using hooks. We'll work with a simple **counter** app that tracks a count and increments the count by 1 when a button is clicked.

Class-Based Component Example:

jsx

```jsx
import React, { Component } from 'react';

class Counter extends Component {
  constructor(props) {
    super(props);
    this.state = {
      count: 0,
    };
  }

  increment = () => {
    this.setState({ count: this.state.count + 1 });
  };

  render() {
    return (
```

```
    <div>
      <h1>Count: {this.state.count}</h1>
      <button
onClick={this.increment}>Increment</button>
    </div>
    );
  }
}


export default Counter;
```

Converting to a Functional Component with Hooks:

jsx

```
import React, { useState } from 'react';


function Counter() {
  const [count, setCount] = useState(0);

  const increment = () => {
    setCount(count + 1);
  };

  return (
    <div>
      <h1>Count: {count}</h1>
      <button
onClick={increment}>Increment</button>
    </div>
  );
```

```
}

export default Counter;
```

Explanation:

- The `Counter` class component is converted into a functional component using the `useState` hook.
- The `count` state is managed using `useState`, and the `increment` function updates the count by calling `setCount`.
- The new functional component is much more concise and easier to read.

11.5 Summary of Key Concepts

- **React Hooks**: Hooks allow functional components to manage state, side effects, and more, making them as powerful as class components.
- **`useState` Hook**: Allows you to add state to functional components. It returns the current state and a function to update it.
- **`useEffect` Hook**: Handles side effects like fetching data, setting up subscriptions, and cleaning up after components.

- **Converting Class to Functional Components**: With hooks, we can easily convert class components into functional ones while maintaining the same functionality.

11.6 Conclusion

In this chapter, we explored **React Hooks**, specifically `useState` and `useEffect`, which enable functional components to manage state and handle side effects. We saw how hooks simplify component logic, reduce boilerplate code, and enhance the overall developer experience.

By converting a class component to a functional one, we demonstrated the power of hooks and how they make React development more efficient and cleaner. Understanding hooks is a fundamental skill for modern React development.

In the next chapter, we will dive deeper into **custom hooks**, where you can encapsulate reusable logic and share stateful logic between components. Let's continue building!

CHAPTER 12

UNDERSTANDING USEEFFECT FOR SIDE EFFECTS

In React, managing **side effects** is a crucial part of building interactive and dynamic applications. Side effects refer to operations that interact with the outside world, such as data fetching, subscriptions, timers, or manually modifying the DOM. React provides the `useEffect` hook to handle these side effects in functional components, offering an elegant way to synchronize your app with external systems or APIs.

In this chapter, we will:

- Understand **what side effects** are and how React handles them.
- Learn how to use the `useEffect` hook for common side effects such as **data fetching** and **updating the DOM**.
- Work through a **real-world example** of fetching data from an API and displaying it in your app.

12.1 What Are Side Effects, and How Does React Handle Them?

In the context of React, a **side effect** is any operation that interacts with external systems or triggers actions that are not directly related to rendering the UI. Some common examples of side effects include:

- **Data fetching**: Making HTTP requests to fetch data from an API or a server.
- **Subscriptions**: Subscribing to events (e.g., WebSocket connections, external state management libraries).
- **Timers**: Setting up intervals or timeouts (e.g., using `setInterval()` or `setTimeout()`).
- **Direct DOM Manipulation**: Accessing and modifying the DOM directly (though React generally handles DOM manipulation automatically).

React encourages you to handle side effects separately from the rendering process. Without this separation, you could risk unwanted behavior, like excessive re-renders or incorrect UI updates. The **useEffect** hook provides a clean and declarative way to manage these side effects in functional components.

12.2 Using the `useEffect` Hook for Side Effects

The **useEffect** hook allows you to perform side effects in your functional components. It is similar to lifecycle methods in class components, like componentDidMount, componentDidUpdate, and componentWillUnmount, but it combines all of them into a single API.

Basic Syntax:

jsx

```
useEffect(() => {
  // Code to run on component mount, update, or
unmount
  return () => {
    // Cleanup code (optional)
  };
}, [dependencies]);
```

- **The effect function**: The function inside useEffect() runs after the component renders. It can perform side effects like data fetching, subscriptions, or DOM manipulations.

- **Dependencies**: The second argument to useEffect is an optional array of dependencies. The effect will only run again if any of the dependencies change. If you pass an empty array ([]), the effect will only run once after the initial render (similar to componentDidMount).

1. Running an Effect Once: `componentDidMount` Equivalent

If you want your effect to run only once after the initial render (for example, to fetch data from an API), you can pass an empty dependency array `[]`.

jsx

```
import React, { useState, useEffect } from 'react';

function DataFetcher() {
  const [data, setData] = useState(null);

  useEffect(() => {
    // Simulating an API call

fetch('https://jsonplaceholder.typicode.com/posts/1')
      .then(response => response.json())
      .then(json => setData(json));
  }, []); // Empty array means this runs only
once after the initial render

  return (
    <div>
      {data ? (
        <div>
          <h1>{data.title}</h1>
```

```
      <p>{data.body}</p>
    </div>
  ) : (
    <p>Loading...</p>
  )}
  </div>
);
}


export default DataFetcher;
```

Explanation:

- **useEffect** fetches data from an API once the component mounts.
- The empty dependency array `[]` ensures that the effect runs only once after the initial render.
- The effect updates the component's state with the fetched data, and React re-renders the component with the new data.

---

2. Running an Effect on State or Props Changes: `componentDidUpdate` Equivalent

If you want to run an effect every time a specific piece of state or a prop changes, you can add that state or prop to the dependency array.

```jsx

import React, { useState, useEffect } from
'react';

function Counter() {
  const [count, setCount] = useState(0);

  useEffect(() => {
    document.title = `Count: ${count}`; // Update
the document title based on `count`
  }, [count]); // The effect runs whenever
`count` changes

  return (
    <div>
      <p>Count: {count}</p>
      <button onClick={() => setCount(count +
1)}>Increment</button>
    </div>
  );
}

export default Counter;
```

Explanation:

- The useEffect hook runs whenever the count state
  changes.

137

- In this example, it updates the document title with the current count.

12.3 Real-World Example: Fetching Data from an API and Displaying It in Your App

---

Now, let's work through a real-world example where we use **useEffect** to fetch data from an API and display it in a React app. We will use the **JSONPlaceholder** API, a free fake online REST API for testing and prototyping.

Step 1: Create the DataFetching Component
jsx

```jsx
import React, { useState, useEffect } from 'react';

function DataFetcher() {
  const [data, setData] = useState(null);
  const [loading, setLoading] = useState(true);

  useEffect(() => {
    // Fetching data from an API

fetch('https://jsonplaceholder.typicode.com/posts')
```

```
.then((response) => response.json())
.then((json) => {
  setData(json);  // Set the fetched data
in state
  setLoading(false);  // Set loading to
false after data is fetched
})
.catch((error) => {
  console.error('Error  fetching  data:',
error);
  setLoading(false);
});
}, []); // Empty dependency array means the
effect runs only once when the component mounts

return (
  <div>
    <h1>Fetched Posts</h1>
    {loading ? (
      <p>Loading...</p>
    ) : (
      <ul>
        {data.map((post) => (
          <li key={post.id}>
            <h3>{post.title}</h3>
            <p>{post.body}</p>
          </li>
        ))}
      </ul>
```

```
    ) }
  </div>
 );
}
```

```
export default DataFetcher;
```

Step 2: Using the `DataFetcher` Component in the App

`jsx`

```
import React from 'react';
import DataFetcher from './DataFetcher';

function App() {
  return (
    <div>
      <h1>My React App</h1>
      <DataFetcher />
    </div>
  );
}
```

```
export default App;
```

Explanation:

- The `DataFetcher` component fetches a list of posts from the **JSONPlaceholder** API using the `fetch` function inside the `useEffect` hook.

- The data is stored in the `data` state, and the `loading` state is used to display a loading message while the data is being fetched.
- Once the data is fetched, the state is updated, and the posts are rendered inside a `<ul>`.

12.4 Cleanup in `useEffect`

React also allows you to **clean up** after your effects. For example, if your component subscribes to a data stream, sets up an event listener, or uses a timer, you should clean up those resources when the component unmounts to avoid memory leaks.

You can return a cleanup function inside `useEffect` that will be called when the component unmounts or before the effect re-runs.

Example: Cleaning up a timer with `clearInterval`.

```jsx
import React, { useState, useEffect } from
'react';

function Timer() {
  const [seconds, setSeconds] = useState(0);
```

```
useEffect(() => {
  const interval = setInterval(() => {
    setSeconds((prevSeconds) => prevSeconds +
1);
  }, 1000);

  // Cleanup the timer when the component
unmounts
  return () => clearInterval(interval);
}, []); // Empty dependency array ensures the
effect runs only once

  return <div>Timer: {seconds} seconds</div>;
}

export default Timer;
```

Explanation:

- We set up an interval using `setInterval` to increment the `seconds` state every second.
- When the component unmounts or before the effect runs again, the cleanup function `clearInterval(interval)` is called to clear the interval.

12.5 Summary of Key Concepts

- **Side Effects**: Operations like data fetching, subscriptions, and timers that interact with external systems and are not related to rendering.

- **useEffect Hook**: Used to handle side effects in functional components. It runs after every render or when specific dependencies change.

- **Data Fetching**: You can use useEffect to fetch data from APIs and update the component's state.

- **Cleanup**: Use the return function inside useEffect to clean up resources, such as timers or event listeners, when the component unmounts.

12.6 Conclusion

In this chapter, we learned how to use the **useEffect** hook to manage **side effects** in React functional components. We explored how useEffect can be used for **data fetching, updating the DOM**, and other side effects that run outside the rendering process. We also covered how to clean up after effects to avoid memory leaks.

Mastering the useEffect hook is crucial for building complex and efficient React applications. In the next chapter, we will look at **custom hooks**, which allow you to extract reusable logic from your components and share it across multiple components. Let's continue building!

CHAPTER 13

USING *useContext* FOR GLOBAL STATE MANAGEMENT

React's **Context API** allows you to manage **global state** without prop drilling, making it an essential tool for large applications. In React, **global state** refers to data that needs to be accessible by multiple components, regardless of how deeply they are nested in the component tree. The `useContext` hook provides an easy way to consume that context and access the global state in functional components.

In this chapter, we will:

- Understand **what React Context is** and when to use it.
- Learn how to use the `useContext` hook to manage global state.
- Build a **real-world example**: A **theme switcher** to toggle between light and dark modes using the Context API.

13.1 What Is React Context and When Should It Be Used?

In React, **Context** provides a way to share **values** (such as data, functions, or settings) across the component tree without passing props manually through every level. It solves the problem of **prop drilling**, where you pass data from parent to child components, and then from child to grandchild components, and so on. This can become cumbersome when many levels of components need access to the same data.

When to use Context:

- **Global State**: When you need to share values like authentication status, user preferences, or theme settings across multiple components.
- **Avoiding Prop Drilling**: When passing props through many levels becomes complicated or inefficient.
- **Shared Functions**: When you need functions (such as toggling a theme, user settings, etc.) to be accessible across the app without having to pass them down manually.

13.2 How to Use `useContext` to Manage Global State

To manage global state using the Context API, there are three main steps:

1. **Create a Context**: Using `React.createContext()`, we define a Context that will store our global state.

2. **Provide the Context**: Use the `Provider` component to make the state available to all components that need it.

3. **Consume the Context**: Use the `useContext` hook to access the global state inside functional components.

Step 1: Create a Context

First, we create a Context object that will hold our global state. The `createContext()` method returns an object with two components: `Provider` and `Consumer`. The `Provider` is used to supply the state, and `useContext` (or `Consumer`) is used to consume the state.

```jsx
import React, { createContext, useState } from 'react';

// Create a Context for the theme
const ThemeContext = createContext();

export default ThemeContext;
```

Explanation:

- ThemeContext will hold the global state for our theme (light or dark).
- createContext() returns an object that includes a Provider and Consumer, which are used to pass and consume the state.

Step 2: Provide the Context

Next, we use the Provider to wrap the component tree where we want the global state to be available. The Provider accepts a value prop, which is the state we want to share.

jsx

```
import React, { useState } from 'react';
import ThemeContext from './ThemeContext';
import ThemeSwitcher from './ThemeSwitcher';
import Content from './Content';

function App() {
  const [theme, setTheme] = useState('light');

  const toggleTheme = () => {
    setTheme((prevTheme)    =>    (prevTheme    ===
'light' ? 'dark' : 'light'));
  };

  return (
```

```
    <ThemeContext.Provider     value={{     theme,
toggleTheme }}>
      <div>
        <h1>Global Theme Switcher</h1>
        <ThemeSwitcher />
        <Content />
      </div>
    </ThemeContext.Provider>
  );
}

export default App;
```

Explanation:

- The `ThemeContext.Provider` wraps the entire component tree. The `value` prop of the `Provider` is an object containing the `theme` state and the `toggleTheme` function, which is used to change the theme.
- Now, any component inside the `Provider` can consume the `theme` and `toggleTheme` values.

Step 3: Consume the Context

To consume the context, we use the `useContext` hook in any component that needs access to the global state. This allows the component to subscribe to the context and automatically re-render when the context value changes.

jsx

```jsx
import React, { useContext } from 'react';
import ThemeContext from './ThemeContext';

function ThemeSwitcher() {
  const { theme, toggleTheme } = useContext(ThemeContext); // Access theme and toggleTheme

  return (
    <div>
      <p>Current theme: {theme}</p>
      <button onClick={toggleTheme}>
        Switch to {theme === 'light' ? 'dark' : 'light'} mode
      </button>
    </div>
  );
}

export default ThemeSwitcher;
```

Explanation:

- The `useContext(ThemeContext)` hook allows the `ThemeSwitcher` component to access the `theme` and `toggleTheme` values provided by the `ThemeContext.Provider`.

- The component displays the current theme and provides a button that toggles the theme when clicked.

Step 4: Display the Themed Content

We also create a `Content` component that will change its style based on the current theme.

jsx

```
import React, { useContext } from 'react';
import ThemeContext from './ThemeContext';

function Content() {
  const { theme } = useContext(ThemeContext); //
Access the current theme

  return (
    <div style={{ background: theme === 'light'
? '#fff' : '#333', color: theme === 'light' ?
'#000' : '#fff' }}>
      <h2>This is the content area</h2>
      <p>The background color changes based on
the current theme.</p>
    </div>
  );
}

export default Content;
```

Explanation:

- The `Content` component uses the current `theme` from the context to adjust its background and text color. The background is white for the light theme and dark for the dark theme.

13.3 Real-World Example: Creating a Theme Switcher with Context API

In this example, we've built a simple **theme switcher** application using the React Context API to manage the global state for the theme (light or dark).

1. **Context Creation**: We created `ThemeContext` to store the theme and the function to toggle it.
2. **Providing State**: The `App` component wrapped the component tree with `ThemeContext.Provider` and passed the theme and toggle function as the context value.
3. **Consuming Context**: The `ThemeSwitcher` and `Content` components used the `useContext` hook to access the `theme` value and update the UI accordingly.

13.4 Summary of Key Concepts

- **React Context** is a powerful feature for managing **global state** in an application without needing to pass props down manually through every level of the component tree.
- `useContext` **Hook** is used to consume context values in functional components.
- **Global State**: The Context API is ideal for managing global state, such as theme settings, authentication status, or language preferences, across an application.
- **Provider and Consumer**: `Provider` supplies the context value to components, and `useContext` or `Consumer` is used to access the context.

13.5 Conclusion

In this chapter, we learned how to use the **React Context API** and the `useContext` **hook** to manage global state in functional components. We explored how to create a global context, provide values using the `Provider`, and consume the context values using the `useContext` hook. By building a **theme switcher**, we demonstrated how React Context can simplify state management and eliminate prop drilling, making your code more maintainable and scalable.

In the next chapter, we will explore **React Router**, which allows you to handle navigation and routing in React applications. Let's continue building!

CHAPTER 14

USEREDUCER – A MORE ADVANCED STATE MANAGEMENT HOOK

While the useState hook is great for managing simple state, managing complex state logic can become challenging in larger applications. When your state logic grows more intricate, such as handling multiple interdependent pieces of state, React's **useReducer** hook becomes a more suitable option. It provides a more structured and scalable way to manage state, especially when there are multiple updates to the state based on different actions.

In this chapter, we will:

- Understand **when to use useReducer** over useState.
- Learn how to manage **complex state logic** with useReducer.
- Build a **real-world example**: A **multi-step form** where the state is managed by useReducer.

14.1 When to Use useReducer Over useState

The **useState** hook is great for managing simple state in functional components, but as your application grows in complexity, you might run into situations where managing state with useState becomes cumbersome.

Here are some scenarios where **useReducer** is a better option:

1. **Complex State Logic**: When the state is an object or an array with multiple fields, and changes to one field depend on the other.

2. **Multiple State Transitions**: When the state needs to undergo multiple updates based on different actions (e.g., updating different parts of state based on different events).

3. **Improved Debugging**: useReducer can make it easier to track state changes in more complex applications, especially when using dev tools like Redux DevTools.

Key Differences Between useState and useReducer:

- **useState**: Good for managing simple state (like a single variable).

- **useReducer**: Ideal for managing complex state logic where the next state depends on the previous one, or when multiple state variables are updated simultaneously.

14.2 Managing Complex State Logic with `useReducer`

useReducer is a hook that is similar to useState, but it gives you more control over how the state is updated. It works by dispatching **actions** to a **reducer function**, which returns a new state based on the action type.

Here's how useReducer works:

jsx

```
const [state, dispatch] = useReducer(reducer,
initialState);
```

- **state**: The current state value.
- **dispatch**: A function that allows you to send actions to the reducer.
- **reducer**: A function that takes the current state and an action, then returns a new state.
- **initialState**: The initial state of your component.

Reducer Function Syntax:

jsx

```
function reducer(state, action) {
  switch (action.type) {
    case 'ACTION_TYPE':
```

157

```
      return { ...state, ...action.payload };
  default:
      return state;
  }
}
```

- The **reducer** function receives the current `state` and an `action` object with a `type` and an optional `payload`.
- Based on the `action.type`, the reducer updates the state and returns the new state.
- The **dispatch** function sends actions to the reducer, triggering state updates.

Example of `useReducer` in Practice:

jsx

```
import React, { useReducer } from 'react';

// Initial state for the counter
const initialState = { count: 0 };

// Reducer function to handle actions
function reducer(state, action) {
  switch (action.type) {
    case 'increment':
      return { count: state.count + 1 };
    case 'decrement':
      return { count: state.count - 1 };
    default:
```

```
      return state;
  }
}

function Counter() {
  // Using useReducer hook
  const [state, dispatch] = useReducer(reducer,
initialState);

  return (
    <div>
      <p>Count: {state.count}</p>
      <button onClick={() => dispatch({ type:
'increment' })}>Increment</button>
      <button onClick={() => dispatch({ type:
'decrement' })}>Decrement</button>
    </div>
  );
}

export default Counter;
```

Explanation:

- We use `useReducer` to manage a counter's state.
- The `reducer` function handles two actions: `'increment'` and `'decrement'`. It updates the `count` based on the action type.

159

- The `dispatch` function is used to trigger actions and update the state accordingly.

14.3 Real-World Example: Creating a Multi-Step Form with State Managed by `useReducer`

Let's now build a **multi-step form** where the state is managed by `useReducer`. Each step will update a different part of the form data, and the final submission will combine all the collected data.

Step 1: Define the Reducer and Initial State

We'll need to manage the form data, including fields like `name`, `email`, and `age`. The state will change step-by-step as the user progresses through the form.

```jsx
import React, { useReducer } from 'react';

// Initial state for the form
const initialState = {
  step: 1,
  name: '',
  email: '',
  age: ''
```

```
};


// Reducer function to handle the form state
function reducer(state, action) {
  switch (action.type) {
    case 'NEXT_STEP':
      return { ...state, step: state.step + 1 };
    case 'PREV_STEP':
      return { ...state, step: state.step - 1 };
    case 'SET_NAME':
      return { ...state, name: action.payload };
    case 'SET_EMAIL':
      return { ...state, email: action.payload };
    case 'SET_AGE':
      return { ...state, age: action.payload };
    case 'SUBMIT':
      return { ...state, step: 4 }; // Show
submission step
    default:
      return state;
  }
}
```

Explanation:

- The initialState includes the step number and form fields (name, email, age).

161

- The `reducer` function handles actions like `NEXT_STEP`, `PREV_STEP`, `SET_NAME`, `SET_EMAIL`, `SET_AGE`, and `SUBMIT`.

Step 2: Create the Multi-Step Form Component

Now, let's create the form with multiple steps. We will render different sections based on the current `step` and update the state with the corresponding actions.

jsx

```
function MultiStepForm() {
  const [state, dispatch] = useReducer(reducer,
initialState);

  const handleSubmit = (event) => {
    event.preventDefault();
    dispatch({ type: 'SUBMIT' });
  };

  return (
    <div>
      <h1>Multi-Step Form</h1>
      <form onSubmit={handleSubmit}>
        {state.step === 1 && (
          <div>
            <label>Name:</label>
            <input
```

```
              type="text"
              value={state.name}
              onChange={(e) => dispatch({ type:
'SET_NAME', payload: e.target.value })}
            />
            <button type="button" onClick={() =>
dispatch({ type: 'NEXT_STEP' })}>
              Next
            </button>
          </div>
        )}

        {state.step === 2 && (
          <div>
            <label>Email:</label>
            <input
              type="email"
              value={state.email}
              onChange={(e) => dispatch({ type:
'SET_EMAIL', payload: e.target.value })}
            />
            <button type="button" onClick={() =>
dispatch({ type: 'PREV_STEP' })}>
              Back
            </button>
            <button type="button" onClick={() =>
dispatch({ type: 'NEXT_STEP' })}>
              Next
            </button>
```

```
      </div>
    )}


    {state.step === 3 && (
      <div>
        <label>Age:</label>
        <input
          type="number"
          value={state.age}
          onChange={(e) => dispatch({ type:
'SET_AGE', payload: e.target.value })}
        />
        <button type="button" onClick={() =>
dispatch({ type: 'PREV_STEP' })}>
          Back
        </button>
        <button
type="submit">Submit</button>
      </div>
    )}


    {state.step === 4 && (
      <div>
        <h2>Form Submitted</h2>
        <p>Name: {state.name}</p>
        <p>Email: {state.email}</p>
        <p>Age: {state.age}</p>
      </div>
    )}
```

```
      </form>
    </div>
  );
}


export default MultiStepForm;
```

Explanation:

- The `MultiStepForm` component displays different sections of the form based on the current `step` in the state.
- The `dispatch` function updates the form fields and moves between steps by dispatching actions (NEXT_STEP, PREV_STEP).
- When the form is submitted, the SUBMIT action is dispatched, and a confirmation step is displayed.

14.4 Summary of Key Concepts

- **useReducer** is a hook used to manage complex state logic in React. It is ideal for situations where state changes involve multiple pieces of data and complex interactions.
- **The Reducer Function**: The `useReducer` hook uses a reducer function to manage the state. This function takes the current state and an action and returns a new state.

165

- **When to Use useReducer**: Use useReducer when managing complex state logic that involves multiple updates or when state needs to be updated in a predictable and centralized way.
- **Real-World Example**: We built a multi-step form where state is managed by useReducer. The state changes based on user interactions, and different sections of the form are rendered based on the current step.

14.5 Conclusion

In this chapter, we explored how **useReducer** can be used to manage complex state logic in React. We learned how to use the reducer function to handle actions and update the state in a predictable way. By building a **multi-step form**, we demonstrated how useReducer can help organize state management in a more structured way.

In the next chapter, we will dive into **React Router** to handle routing and navigation in your React applications. Let's continue building!

CHAPTER 15

REACT ROUTER FOR NAVIGATION

One of the most essential aspects of building dynamic web applications is **navigation**. In traditional multi-page applications (MPAs), each page is loaded from the server as the user clicks a link. However, in modern **single-page applications** (SPAs), navigation happens without reloading the entire page. This seamless navigation is handled by libraries like **React Router**.

In this chapter, we will:

- Introduce **React Router** and understand why it is important for SPAs.
- Learn how to set up **routes** and implement **link navigation** in React.
- Build a **real-world example**: A **blog** with multiple pages (home, post details, and about) using React Router.

15.1 Introduction to React Router for Handling Navigation in Single-Page Applications

In single-page applications (SPAs), React Router allows you to navigate between different views (or pages) without refreshing the entire page. Instead of using traditional full-page reloads, React Router updates the browser's URL and dynamically changes the content without reloading the page. This results in a smoother, faster user experience.

Key Features of React Router:

- **Declarative routing**: You define the routes and which components should be rendered for each route.
- **Dynamic routing**: Routes are rendered dynamically as the app loads, which makes the app feel faster.
- **History manipulation**: React Router works with the browser's history API to update the URL and manage navigation history.
- **Nested routing**: You can nest routes, meaning you can have routes within routes, providing a flexible routing structure.

React Router is widely used for **navigation management** in SPAs, making it an essential tool for React developers.

15.2 Setting Up Routes and Link Navigation

To get started with React Router, you need to install the package:

bash

npm install react-router-dom

Once installed, you can begin setting up your routes and links.

1. Setting Up the Router

To define routes, you need to wrap your app with the BrowserRouter component, which provides the routing context to the entire application.

jsx

```jsx
import React from 'react';
import { BrowserRouter as Router, Route, Switch
} from 'react-router-dom';
import Home from './Home';
import Post from './Post';
import About from './About';

function App() {
  return (
    <Router>
      <div>
        <h1>My Blog</h1>
        <nav>
          <ul>
            <li>
              <Link to="/">Home</Link>
```

169

```
        </li>
        <li>
          <Link to="/about">About</Link>
        </li>
      </ul>
    </nav>

    <Switch>
        <Route path="/" exact component={Home}
/>
        <Route                    path="/post/:id"
component={Post} />
        <Route path="/about" component={About}
/>
      </Switch>
    </div>
  </Router>
  );
}


export default App;
```

Explanation:

- **BrowserRouter**: Wraps the entire app to enable routing functionality.
- **Route**: Defines a path and the component to render when the URL matches that path. You can specify the exact path or use dynamic routes like /post/:id.

170

- **Link**: Used for navigation between pages. Link components replace traditional anchor (<a>) tags and do not trigger a page reload.
- **Switch**: Ensures that only one Route is rendered at a time. It renders the first route that matches the current location.

2. Dynamic Routes with URL Parameters

React Router allows you to create **dynamic routes** where parts of the URL can be variables. You can access these variables in the component using props.match.params.

```jsx

import React from 'react';
import { useParams } from 'react-router-dom';

function Post() {
  const { id } = useParams(); // Access dynamic
part of the URL
  return <div>Post ID: {id}</div>;
}

export default Post;
```

Explanation:

- In this case, the `Post` component gets the `id` of the post from the URL (e.g., `/post/1`) and displays it dynamically.

3. Navigating Programmatically

You can also navigate programmatically using the `useHistory` hook from `react-router-dom` to push new routes.

jsx

```jsx
import React from 'react';
import { useHistory } from 'react-router-dom';

function NavigateButton() {
  const history = useHistory();

  const navigateToPost = (id) => {
    history.push(`/post/${id}`);
  };

  return (
    <button onClick={() => navigateToPost(1)}>
      Go to Post 1
    </button>
  );
}

export default NavigateButton;
```

Explanation:

- The useHistory hook gives you access to the browser's history, and you can programmatically navigate to different routes using history.push().
- In this example, clicking the button navigates to /post/1.

15.3 Real-World Example: Creating a Blog with Multiple Pages Using React Router

Now that we understand how React Router works, let's build a simple **blog** with three pages:

- **Home page**: Displays a list of blog posts.
- **Post page**: Displays an individual post.
- **About page**: Displays information about the blog.

Step 1: Create the Components

First, let's create the basic components for Home, Post, and About.

Home Component (Home.js):

jsx

173

```jsx
import React from 'react';
import { Link } from 'react-router-dom';

function Home() {
  return (
    <div>
      <h2>Home Page</h2>
      <ul>
        <li>
          <Link to="/post/1">Post 1</Link>
        </li>
        <li>
          <Link to="/post/2">Post 2</Link>
        </li>
      </ul>
    </div>
  );
}

export default Home;
```

Post Component (Post.js):

jsx

```jsx
import React from 'react';
import { useParams } from 'react-router-dom';

function Post() {
```

```
  const { id } = useParams();

  return (
    <div>
      <h2>Post {id}</h2>
      <p>This is the content for post {id}.</p>
    </div>
  );
}


export default Post;
```

About Component (About.js):

jsx

```
import React from 'react';


function About() {
  return (
    <div>
      <h2>About Page</h2>
      <p>This is a simple blog built with React
and React Router.</p>
    </div>
  );
}


export default About;
```

Step 2: Put Everything Together in the App Component

Now, let's tie everything together in the `App.js` file by using `BrowserRouter`, `Route`, `Link`, and `Switch` for navigation.

jsx

```
import React from 'react';
import { BrowserRouter as Router, Route, Switch,
Link } from 'react-router-dom';
import Home from './Home';
import Post from './Post';
import About from './About';

function App() {
  return (
    <Router>
      <div>
        <h1>My Blog</h1>
        <nav>
          <ul>
            <li><Link to="/">Home</Link></li>
            <li><Link
to="/about">About</Link></li>
          </ul>
        </nav>

        <Switch>
```

```
        <Route path="/" exact component={Home}
/>
        <Route           path="/post/:id"
component={Post} />
        <Route path="/about" component={About}
/>
      </Switch>
    </div>
  </Router>
  );
}

export default App;
```

Explanation:

- The `Router` component wraps the entire app to enable routing.

- The `Switch` component ensures that only one `Route` is rendered based on the current URL.

- The `Link` component provides navigation to different routes without reloading the page.

15.4 Summary of Key Concepts

- **React Router**: A library that enables navigation in React applications without reloading the page. It helps build SPAs by managing routes and links.
- **BrowserRouter**: A wrapper that provides routing context to the app.
- **Route**: Defines a path and the component to render when the URL matches that path.
- **Link**: Used for navigating between pages in the app without reloading the page.
- **Dynamic Routing**: React Router allows dynamic routes using URL parameters (e.g., /post/:id).
- **Programmatic Navigation**: Use useHistory to navigate programmatically to different routes.
- **Switch**: Ensures that only the first matching route is rendered.

15.5 Conclusion

In this chapter, we learned how to use **React Router** to handle navigation in single-page applications. We explored how to set up routes, use Link components for navigation, and manage dynamic routes with URL parameters. By building a simple **blog** with multiple pages, we demonstrated how React Router can simplify navigation in React applications.

In the next chapter, we will explore **React Forms** and how to manage form data and validation in React apps. Let's continue building!

CHAPTER 16

FETCHING DATA WITH `FETCH()` AND `AXIOS`

One of the core features of modern web applications is the ability to interact with external data sources, typically via **HTTP requests**. React, being a client-side JavaScript library, allows you to fetch data from external APIs and display it within your application. In this chapter, we will learn about two common methods for making HTTP requests in React: `fetch()` and `axios`.

We will also cover how **asynchronous code** works in React, particularly using **Promises** and **async/await** syntax, which is essential for handling requests that take time, such as fetching data from a public API.

By the end of this chapter, you will have the skills to fetch data from an API and integrate it into your React components, providing dynamic and real-time content to users.

16.1 Introduction to `fetch()` and `axios` for Making HTTP Requests

There are two primary ways to make HTTP requests in React: using the built-in **`fetch()`** function or the third-party **`axios`** library. Both have their advantages, and the choice depends on your specific needs.

1. Using `fetch()`

`fetch()` is a native JavaScript function for making HTTP requests. It returns a **Promise** that resolves to the **Response** object representing the response to the request. By default, `fetch()` does not throw an error for HTTP error statuses (like 404 or 500), so you need to manually check the response status.

Example of `fetch()`:

jsx

```
fetch('https://jsonplaceholder.typicode.com/pos
ts')
    .then((response) => response.json())
    .then((data) => console.log(data))
    .catch((error)       =>        console.error('Error
fetching data:', error));
```

- **fetch()** returns a **Promise** that resolves to the response object.
- **response.json()** converts the response into JSON format.

2. Using axios

axios is a popular third-party library for making HTTP requests. It simplifies requests, automatically converts the response to JSON, and handles errors more gracefully than fetch(). Additionally, axios supports features like request cancellation, custom headers, and better error handling out of the box.

Example of axios:

bash

```
npm install axios
```
jsx

```
import axios from 'axios';

axios.get('https://jsonplaceholder.typicode.com/posts')
  .then((response)                              =>
console.log(response.data))
  .catch((error)      =>      console.error('Error
fetching data:', error));
```

- **axios.get()** is used to make a GET request. It automatically parses the response into JSON.
- The data is available directly on `response.data`, simplifying the code.

Both methods (`fetch()` and `axios`) allow you to make asynchronous HTTP requests, but `axios` tends to be easier to use and provides additional features.

16.2 Understanding How Asynchronous Code Works in React

When making HTTP requests, you are working with **asynchronous** code, meaning the request is made in the background and does not block the rest of your program. React uses **Promises** to handle asynchronous code, allowing you to handle successful responses and errors separately.

1. Promises

A **Promise** is an object that represents the eventual completion (or failure) of an asynchronous operation and its resulting value. You can handle the result of a Promise using the `then()` and `catch()` methods.

jsx

```
fetch('https://jsonplaceholder.typicode.com/pos
ts')
  .then((response)  =>  response.json())      //
Converts the response to JSON
  .then((data) => {
    console.log(data);  // Use the data from the
API
  })
  .catch((error) => {
    console.error('Error:', error);   // Handle
errors
  });
```

- **then()**: Called when the Promise resolves successfully.
- **catch()**: Called when the Promise is rejected due to an error.

2. Async/Await Syntax

React also supports the **async/await** syntax, which allows you to write asynchronous code in a synchronous-looking manner, making it easier to read and understand.

```jsx
async function fetchData() {
  try {
```

```
    const        response        =        await
fetch('https://jsonplaceholder.typicode.com/pos
ts');
    const data = await response.json();
    console.log(data);  // Use the data from the
API
  } catch (error) {
    console.error('Error:', error);   // Handle
errors
  }
}
```

- **async**: Marks the function as asynchronous.
- **await**: Waits for the Promise to resolve before proceeding to the next line of code.

Using `async/await` makes the code easier to read and maintain, especially when you have multiple asynchronous operations.

16.3 Real-World Example: Fetching Data from a Public API and Displaying It in Your App

---

Now that we understand how to use `fetch()` and `axios` for making HTTP requests and how to work with asynchronous code, let's put it all together in a real-world example. In this example, we will fetch data from a public API (JSONPlaceholder) and display it in our React app.

Step 1: Create a Component to Fetch and Display Data

Let's create a component called **PostList** that fetches a list of posts and displays them.

jsx

```
import React, { useState, useEffect } from
'react';

function PostList() {
  const [posts, setPosts] = useState([]);
  const [loading, setLoading] = useState(true);
  const [error, setError] = useState(null);

  // Fetch data when the component mounts
  useEffect(() => {
    const fetchPosts = async () => {
      try {
        const        response       =        await
fetch('https://jsonplaceholder.typicode.com/pos
ts');
        const data = await response.json();
        setPosts(data);
      } catch (err) {
        setError('Failed to fetch posts');
```

```
    } finally {
      setLoading(false);
    }
  };

  fetchPosts();
}, []); // Empty dependency array means the
effect runs only once when the component mounts

  // Display loading state, error state, or posts
  if (loading) return <p>Loading...</p>;
  if (error) return <p>{error}</p>;

  return (
    <div>
      <h1>Posts</h1>
      <ul>
        {posts.map((post) => (
          <li key={post.id}>
            <h2>{post.title}</h2>
            <p>{post.body}</p>
          </li>
        ))}
      </ul>
    </div>
  );
}

export default PostList;
```

187

Explanation:

- **State Management**: We use the `useState` hook to manage the `posts`, `loading`, and `error` states.
- **Data Fetching with `useEffect`**: The `useEffect` hook is used to fetch data when the component mounts. The `async/await` syntax is used for cleaner and more readable asynchronous code.
- **Handling Loading and Error**: We display a loading message while fetching data, and an error message if the request fails.

Step 2: Use the PostList Component in Your App

Now, let's render the `PostList` component inside the main `App` component.

jsx

```
import React from 'react';
import PostList from './PostList';

function App() {
  return (
    <div>
      <h1>React Data Fetching Example</h1>
      <PostList />
    </div>
```

```
  );
}
```

```
export default App;
```

16.4 Summary of Key Concepts

- **fetch()** and **axios** are both commonly used methods for making HTTP requests in React. fetch() is built-in, while axios is a third-party library with additional features.
- **Asynchronous Code**: React makes use of **Promises** and **async/await** to handle asynchronous operations like HTTP requests.
- **useEffect**: Use the useEffect hook to fetch data when the component mounts.
- **State Management**: Use React state (useState) to store and display the fetched data, and handle loading and error states effectively.

16.5 Conclusion

In this chapter, we learned how to fetch data from external APIs using fetch() and axios in React. We also explored how asynchronous operations work in React using **Promises** and **async/await**. Finally, we built a real-world example of a **PostList** component that fetches and displays a list of posts from a public API.

In the next chapter, we will dive deeper into **state management** with **Redux** and explore how to manage more complex state logic in larger applications. Let's continue building!

CHAPTER 17

INTEGRATING REST APIS IN REACT

In modern web applications, it's common to interact with **RESTful APIs** to fetch, update, or delete data. React, as a client-side JavaScript library, makes it easy to interact with these APIs and display the data in your components. Understanding how to fetch and manage data from a REST API is crucial for building dynamic and data-driven React applications.

In this chapter, we will:

- **Understand RESTful services** and how React interacts with them.
- Learn how to **manage API responses** and handle **error handling** in React.
- Build a **real-world weather app** that fetches data from a weather API and displays it.

17.1 Understanding RESTful Services and How React Interacts with Them

191

REST (Representational State Transfer) is an architectural style for designing networked applications. A **RESTful API** allows clients (like React applications) to interact with server resources using standard HTTP methods such as **GET**, **POST**, **PUT**, and **DELETE**.

RESTful HTTP Methods:

- **GET**: Fetches data from the server (e.g., fetching weather information).
- **POST**: Sends data to the server to create a new resource (e.g., submitting a form).
- **PUT**: Updates an existing resource on the server.
- **DELETE**: Removes a resource from the server.

React interacts with REST APIs mainly by making **HTTP requests** using the `fetch()` function or libraries like `axios`. These requests are typically **asynchronous**, meaning they happen in the background without blocking the main application thread.

How React Makes HTTP Requests:

- We use `fetch()` or `axios` to send requests to a RESTful API.
- The response is usually in **JSON** format, which can then be parsed and displayed in the React component.
- You can manage API responses by using **state** in React to store the data and **update the UI** once the data is fetched.

192

17.2 Managing API Responses and Error Handling

When interacting with APIs, it is crucial to handle both **successful responses** and **errors** gracefully. This ensures that users are informed if something goes wrong (e.g., no network connection, or an invalid response from the API).

1. Handling Successful Responses

After making an API request, we typically process the data and update the component's state to reflect the changes.

jsx

```
fetch('https://api.openweathermap.org/data/2.5/
weather?q=London&appid=YOUR_API_KEY')
  .then(response => response.json())
  .then(data => {
    // Update state with API data
    console.log(data);
  })
  .catch(error => {
    // Handle error
    console.error('Error    fetching    data:',
error);
  });
```

2. Error Handling

To ensure a robust user experience, it's important to handle **network errors** and **API errors**. The `fetch()` function doesn't reject an HTTP error response (e.g., 404 or 500), so you need to manually check the response status.

jsx

```jsx
fetch('https://api.openweathermap.org/data/2.5/
weather?q=London&appid=YOUR_API_KEY')
  .then(response => {
    if (!response.ok) {
      throw new Error('Network response was not
ok');
    }
    return response.json();
  })
  .then(data => {
    console.log(data);
  })
  .catch(error => {
    console.error('Error:', error);
  });
```

3. Handling Loading and Error States in React

In React, it's common to show a **loading indicator** while waiting for the data and an **error message** if something goes wrong. You can use **state** to track these conditions.

jsx

```
const [weather, setWeather] = useState(null);
const [loading, setLoading] = useState(true);
const [error, setError] = useState(null);

useEffect(() => {

fetch('https://api.openweathermap.org/data/2.5/
weather?q=London&appid=YOUR_API_KEY')
    .then(response => {
      if (!response.ok) {
        throw new Error('Network response was not
ok');
      }
      return response.json();
    })
    .then(data => {
      setWeather(data);
      setLoading(false);
    })
    .catch(error => {
      setError(error.message);
      setLoading(false);
    });
}, []);
```

Explanation:

195

- **Loading state**: Initially, the `loading` state is set to `true`, indicating that the data is being fetched. Once the data is fetched, `loading` is set to `false`.
- **Error state**: If there's an issue with fetching the data, we set the `error` state and display the error message.

17.3 Real-World Example: Building a Weather App that Fetches Data from an API

Now, let's apply what we've learned and build a **weather app** that fetches data from the **OpenWeatherMap API**. We will:

1. Fetch weather data based on a city.
2. Display the weather information.
3. Handle loading and error states.

Step 1: Create a Weather Component

jsx

```
import React, { useState, useEffect } from
'react';

function WeatherApp() {
  const [city, setCity] = useState('London');
  const [weather, setWeather] = useState(null);
  const [loading, setLoading] = useState(true);
```

```
const [error, setError] = useState(null);

useEffect(() => {
  setLoading(true);

fetch(`https://api.openweathermap.org/data/2.5/
weather?q=${city}&appid=YOUR_API_KEY`)
    .then(response => {
      if (!response.ok) {
        throw new Error('City not found');
      }
      return response.json();
    })
    .then(data => {
      setWeather(data);
      setLoading(false);
    })
    .catch(err => {
      setError(err.message);
      setLoading(false);
    });
}, [city]); // Dependency array to re-fetch
when `city` changes

const handleCityChange = (event) => {
  setCity(event.target.value);
};

return (
```

197

```
    <div>
      <h1>Weather App</h1>
      <input
        type="text"
        value={city}
        onChange={handleCityChange}
        placeholder="Enter city"
      />
      {loading && <p>Loading...</p>}
      {error && <p style={{ color: 'red'
}}>{error}</p>}
      {weather && !loading && !error && (
        <div>
          <h2>{weather.name}</h2>

<p>{weather.weather[0].description}</p>
          <p>Temperature: {(weather.main.temp -
273.15).toFixed(2)}°C</p>
          <p>Humidity:
{weather.main.humidity}%</p>
        </div>
      )}
    </div>
  );
}


export default WeatherApp;
```

Explanation:

- We use the `useState` hook to store the `city`, `weather` data, `loading` state, and `error` message.
- The `useEffect` hook runs whenever the `city` changes and fetches weather data from the OpenWeatherMap API.
- If there's an error (e.g., city not found), we display an error message.
- If the data is fetched successfully, we display the weather information including the city name, weather description, temperature, and humidity.

Step 2: Set Up the App Component

jsx

```jsx
import React from 'react';
import WeatherApp from './WeatherApp';

function App() {
  return (
    <div>
      <WeatherApp />
    </div>
  );
}

export default App;
```

- **RESTful APIs**: REST APIs allow you to interact with server resources using standard HTTP methods (GET, POST, etc.).

- **Fetching Data in React**: You can use `fetch()` or `axios` to make HTTP requests in React. `fetch()` returns a **Promise** and requires manual error handling, while `axios` simplifies error handling and automatically parses the response as JSON.

- **Error Handling**: Always handle errors gracefully when fetching data, especially network issues or invalid responses.

- **State Management**: Use `useState` to manage data, loading, and error states, and `useEffect` to fetch data when the component mounts or when a specific state changes.

- **Asynchronous Code**: Use **Promises** or **async/await** to handle asynchronous operations and ensure smooth UI rendering.

17.5 Conclusion

In this chapter, we learned how to integrate **RESTful APIs** into React applications by making HTTP requests using `fetch()` and `axios`. We also explored how to handle **loading, error states**, and **API responses** efficiently. Finally, we built a **weather app** that fetches data from an API and displays it to the user.

In the next chapter, we will dive into **React's Context API** for managing global state and avoiding prop drilling. Let's continue

CHAPTER 18

HANDLING AUTHENTICATION IN REACT

Authentication is one of the most critical aspects of building modern web applications. React, being a client-side library, doesn't have a built-in solution for authentication. However, integrating **authentication** and managing user sessions can be done effectively using a combination of **tokens**, **cookies**, and **local storage**.

In this chapter, we will:

- Understand how to set up **user authentication** in React applications.
- Learn how to work with **tokens**, **cookies**, and **local storage** to manage authentication.
- Build a **real-world example**: A **login system** that uses **JWT (JSON Web Tokens)** for secure authentication.

18.1 Setting Up User Authentication in React Applications

Authentication in React often involves verifying the user's identity and granting access to specific resources or parts of the application. This process is typically done through a server-side API, which validates the user's credentials (like username and password) and returns an authentication token, such as a **JWT** (JSON Web Token).

Key Steps in Authentication:

1. **Login Process**: The user submits their credentials (e.g., username and password) through a login form.
2. **Token Generation**: The server validates the credentials and returns a token (usually a JWT).
3. **Token Storage**: The client (React app) stores the token in a secure place (e.g., local storage or cookies).
4. **Protected Routes**: The client uses the token to make authenticated requests and access protected resources.
5. **Logout**: The user logs out, and the token is removed from storage.

18.2 Working with Tokens, Cookies, and Local Storage for Authentication

To manage authentication in React, the most common approach is to store authentication tokens in either **localStorage**,

sessionStorage, or **cookies**. Each of these storage methods has different characteristics:

1. **localStorage**: Stores data persistently across browser sessions. However, it is accessible through JavaScript, so it's susceptible to cross-site scripting (XSS) attacks. It's suitable for storing non-sensitive data, but sensitive data like JWT should be stored carefully.

2. **sessionStorage**: Similar to `localStorage`, but the data is cleared when the browser or tab is closed. It's used for session-specific data.

3. **Cookies**: Used to store small pieces of data that are sent to the server with every HTTP request. Cookies can be made **HTTP-only** to protect them from JavaScript access, making them more secure against XSS attacks.

Storing Tokens in localStorage

jsx

```
// After successful login, store the token in localStorage
localStorage.setItem('authToken',    'your-jwt-token');
```

Storing Tokens in Cookies

To store a token in cookies with **JavaScript**:

jsx

```
document.cookie = "authToken=your-jwt-token;
path=/; secure; HttpOnly";
```

Note: The HttpOnly flag ensures the cookie is not accessible via JavaScript, providing more security.

Accessing Tokens

To access a stored token in localStorage:

jsx

```
const token = localStorage.getItem('authToken');
```

To access a stored token in cookies:

jsx

```
const getCookie = (name) => {
  const value = `; ${document.cookie}`;
  const parts = value.split(`; ${name}=`);
  if    (parts.length    ===    2)    return
parts.pop().split(';').shift();
};
const token = getCookie('authToken');
```

205

18.3 Real-World Example: Building a Login System with React and JWT

In this section, we will build a **login system** in React that communicates with a server-side API to authenticate the user using **JWT** (JSON Web Tokens). We will use **localStorage** to store the JWT for session management.

Step 1: Set Up the Server API

For simplicity, let's assume you have a backend API that accepts a **POST request** to /login with a username and password and returns a **JWT token** if the credentials are correct.

Example API Response:

```json
json

{
  "token": "your-jwt-token"
}
```

Step 2: Create the Login Form

Let's start by creating a basic login form that accepts **username** and **password**.

206

```jsx

import React, { useState } from 'react';
import { useHistory } from 'react-router-dom';

function Login() {
  const [username, setUsername] = useState('');
  const [password, setPassword] = useState('');
  const [error, setError] = useState('');
  const history = useHistory();

  const handleLogin = async (event) => {
    event.preventDefault();

    try {
      const response = await fetch('https://your-api.com/login', {
        method: 'POST',
        headers: {
          'Content-Type': 'application/json',
        },
        body: JSON.stringify({ username, password }),
      });

      const data = await response.json();

      if (response.ok) {
        // Save the token in localStorage
```

207

```
      localStorage.setItem('authToken',
data.token);


      // Redirect to the dashboard page
      history.push('/dashboard');
    } else {
      // Show error if login fails
      setError(data.message      ||      'Login
failed');
    }
  } catch (error) {
    setError('An error occurred while logging
in');
    }
  };


  return (
    <div>
      <h2>Login</h2>
      <form onSubmit={handleLogin}>
        <div>
          <label>Username:</label>
          <input
            type="text"
            value={username}
            onChange={(e)                =>
setUsername(e.target.value)}
            required
          />
```

```
    </div>
    <div>
      <label>Password:</label>
      <input
        type="password"
        value={password}
        onChange={(e)                    =>
setPassword(e.target.value)}
        required
      />
    </div>
    <button type="submit">Login</button>
  </form>
  {error  &&  <p  style={{  color:  'red'
}}>{error}</p>}
  </div>
  );
}


export default Login;
```

Explanation:

- We use useState to store the username, password, and error messages.
- The handleLogin function sends the login data to the backend API.
- If the login is successful, the **JWT token** is stored in localStorage, and the user is redirected to the

209

/dashboard **page** using useHistory **from React Router.**

- If an error occurs, it is displayed on the screen.

Step 3: Create a Protected Route (Dashboard)

Once the user logs in successfully, we will redirect them to a **dashboard** page. This page should be **protected** and accessible only if the user is authenticated (i.e., if the token is present in localStorage).

jsx

```
import React from 'react';
import { Redirect } from 'react-router-dom';

function Dashboard() {
  const                 token                 =
localStorage.getItem('authToken');

  if (!token) {
    // If no token is found, redirect to login
page
    return <Redirect to="/login" />;
  }

  return (
    <div>
```

```
    <h2>Dashboard</h2>
    <p>Welcome to your dashboard!</p>
  </div>
);
}
```

```
export default Dashboard;
```

Explanation:

- The `Dashboard` component checks if a valid `authToken` is stored in `localStorage`.
- If no token is found, the user is redirected to the login page using `<Redirect />` from React Router.
- If the token is found, the dashboard content is displayed.

Step 4: Create the Logout Functionality

To complete the authentication flow, let's create a **logout** function that removes the JWT token from `localStorage` and redirects the user to the login page.

```
jsx
```

```jsx
import React from 'react';
import { useHistory } from 'react-router-dom';

function Logout() {
```

```
const history = useHistory();

const handleLogout = () => {
  // Remove the token from localStorage
  localStorage.removeItem('authToken');

  // Redirect to login page
  history.push('/login');
};

  return                                <button
onClick={handleLogout}>Logout</button>;
}

export default Logout;
```

Explanation:

- The `handleLogout` function removes the JWT token from `localStorage` and redirects the user back to the login page.

18.4 Summary of Key Concepts

- **JWT (JSON Web Tokens)**: A popular method for authenticating users in web applications. It is a secure way to transmit information between the client and the server.

- **Token Storage**: Tokens can be stored in `localStorage` or cookies. `localStorage` is commonly used for storing session tokens in client-side applications.

- **React Router for Redirects**: We use **React Router's** `<Redirect />` component to protect routes and redirect users based on authentication.

- **Login and Logout**: We built a simple login system where the user authenticates with a username and password, stores the JWT token, and accesses protected pages.

18.5 Conclusion

In this chapter, we learned how to implement **user authentication** in a React application using **JWT (JSON Web Tokens)**. We explored how to handle login, manage tokens in **localStorage**, protect routes with React Router, and implement logout functionality. By building this **login system**, you now have the tools to secure your React applications and manage user sessions.

In the next chapter, we will explore **error boundaries** in React, a powerful tool to catch and handle JavaScript errors in your components. Let's continue building!

CHAPTER 19

WORKING WITH FORMS AND APIS FOR CRUD OPERATIONS

CRUD (Create, Read, Update, Delete) operations are fundamental to most web applications. React allows you to handle these operations effectively by interacting with APIs and managing user input through **forms**. In this chapter, we will explore how to use forms to collect user input and perform CRUD operations in React by interacting with APIs.

We will break down the chapter into:

- How to perform **Create**, **Read**, **Update**, and **Delete** operations in React.
- How to use **forms** for capturing user input and interacting with external APIs.
- **Real-world example**: Building a basic **task management app** with CRUD functionality, where users can create, read, update, and delete tasks.

19.1 Performing Create, Read, Update, and Delete (CRUD) Operations in React

1. Create Operation

The **Create** operation allows users to add new data to the application. In React, this typically involves submitting a form where the user provides input, and then sending the data to the backend API.

Example (Create):

jsx

```jsx
const handleSubmit = (event) => {
  event.preventDefault();
  const newTask = { title: taskTitle };



fetch('https://jsonplaceholder.typicode.com/pos
ts', {
    method: 'POST',
    headers: {
      'Content-Type': 'application/json',
    },
    body: JSON.stringify(newTask),
  })
    .then((response) => response.json())
```

```
   .then((data) => {
     console.log('Task created:', data);
     // Optionally, update state to reflect the
new task
   })
   .catch((error)  =>  console.error('Error:',
error));
};
```

2. Read Operation

The **Read** operation is used to fetch data from the backend. This could be data to display a list of items, such as tasks in a to-do list.

Example (Read):

jsx

```
useEffect(() => {

fetch('https://jsonplaceholder.typicode.com/pos
ts')
   .then((response) => response.json())
   .then((data)  =>  setTasks(data)) // Store
tasks in state
   .catch((error)    =>    console.error('Error
fetching tasks:', error));
}, []); // Run once when the component mounts
```

3. Update Operation

The **Update** operation allows users to modify existing data. This typically involves sending a PUT or PATCH request to the server to update an existing resource.

Example (Update):

jsx

```
const handleUpdate = (taskId, updatedTitle) => {
  const updatedTask = { title: updatedTitle };


fetch(`https://jsonplaceholder.typicode.com/pos
ts/${taskId}`, {
    method: 'PUT',
    headers: {
      'Content-Type': 'application/json',
    },
    body: JSON.stringify(updatedTask),
  })
    .then((response) => response.json())
    .then((data) => {
      console.log('Task updated:', data);
      // Optionally, update state to reflect the
updated task
    })
```

```
    .catch((error)      =>      console.error('Error
updating task:', error));
};
```

4. Delete Operation

The **Delete** operation removes data from the server. In React, this usually involves a button or action that triggers a DELETE request.

Example (Delete):

jsx

```
const handleDelete = (taskId) => {

fetch(`https://jsonplaceholder.typicode.com/pos
ts/${taskId}`, {
    method: 'DELETE',
  })
    .then(() => {
      console.log('Task deleted');
      // Optionally, update state to remove the
deleted task
    })
    .catch((error)      =>      console.error('Error
deleting task:', error));
};
```

19.2 Using Forms to Handle User Input and Interact with APIs

In React, forms are used to collect user input. You can manage form data using **state** and send it to the server via **API requests**. Here, we will demonstrate how to handle form data for **creating tasks** in our task management app.

1. Creating a Task Form

jsx

```jsx
import React, { useState } from 'react';

function TaskForm({ onSubmit }) {
  const [taskTitle, setTaskTitle] = useState('');

  const handleChange = (event) => {
    setTaskTitle(event.target.value);
  };

  const handleSubmit = (event) => {
    event.preventDefault();
    onSubmit(taskTitle); // Pass taskTitle to parent component
    setTaskTitle(''); // Clear the form field
  };

  return (
```

```
    <form onSubmit={handleSubmit}>
      <label>
        Task Title:
        <input    type="text"    value={taskTitle}
onChange={handleChange} />
      </label>
      <button type="submit">Add Task</button>
    </form>
  );
}


export default TaskForm;
```

Explanation:

- `TaskForm` is a simple form that accepts a task title.
- The state `taskTitle` is updated as the user types in the input field.
- When the form is submitted, the `onSubmit` callback is called, passing the task title to the parent component.

2. Using the Form to Create Tasks in the Parent Component
jsx

```
import  React,  {  useState,  useEffect  }  from
'react';
import TaskForm from './TaskForm';


function TaskManager() {
```

```
  const [tasks, setTasks] = useState([]);
  const [loading, setLoading] = useState(true);

  useEffect(() => {

fetch('https://jsonplaceholder.typicode.com/pos
ts')
      .then((response) => response.json())
      .then((data) => {
        setTasks(data);
        setLoading(false);
      })
      .catch((error)   =>   console.error('Error
fetching tasks:', error));
  }, []);

  const handleAddTask = (taskTitle) => {
    const newTask = { title: taskTitle };


fetch('https://jsonplaceholder.typicode.com/pos
ts', {
      method: 'POST',
      headers:           {          'Content-Type':
'application/json' },
      body: JSON.stringify(newTask),
    })
      .then((response) => response.json())
```

221

```
      .then((data)   =>   setTasks((prevTasks)   =>
[...prevTasks, data]))
      .catch((error)   =>   console.error('Error
adding task:', error));
  };

  return (
    <div>
      <h1>Task Manager</h1>
      <TaskForm onSubmit={handleAddTask} />
      {loading ? (
        <p>Loading tasks...</p>
      ) : (
        <ul>
          {tasks.map((task) => (
            <li key={task.id}>{task.title}</li>
          ))}
        </ul>
      )}
    </div>
  );
}

export default TaskManager;
```

Explanation:

- `TaskManager` is the parent component that manages the list of tasks.

- It uses the `useEffect` hook to fetch tasks from the API when the component mounts.
- The `handleAddTask` function is passed to the `TaskForm` component to create new tasks by sending a **POST request** to the API.
- After a new task is successfully added, it updates the list of tasks by appending the new task.

19.3 Real-World Example: Building a Basic Task Management App with CRUD Functionality

---

Now that we have all the building blocks for performing **CRUD** operations, let's combine everything into a simple **task management app**. This app will allow users to:

- **Create** tasks via a form.
- **Read** tasks by fetching them from an API.
- **Update** tasks by editing their titles.
- **Delete** tasks.

Complete Example:

jsx

```
import React, { useState, useEffect } from
'react';
```

```
function TaskForm({ onSubmit }) {
  const     [taskTitle,      setTaskTitle]      =
useState('');

  const handleChange = (event) => {
    setTaskTitle(event.target.value);
  };

  const handleSubmit = (event) => {
    event.preventDefault();
    onSubmit(taskTitle);
    setTaskTitle('');
  };

  return (
    <form onSubmit={handleSubmit}>
      <label>
        Task Title:
        <input    type="text"    value={taskTitle}
onChange={handleChange} />
      </label>
      <button type="submit">Add Task</button>
    </form>
  );
}

function TaskManager() {
  const [tasks, setTasks] = useState([]);
  const [loading, setLoading] = useState(true);
```

```
  useEffect(() => {

fetch('https://jsonplaceholder.typicode.com/pos
ts')
      .then((response) => response.json())
      .then((data) => {
        setTasks(data);
        setLoading(false);
      })
      .catch((error)    =>    console.error('Error
fetching tasks:', error));
  }, []);

  const handleAddTask = (taskTitle) => {
    const newTask = { title: taskTitle };


fetch('https://jsonplaceholder.typicode.com/pos
ts', {
      method: 'POST',
      headers:           {          'Content-Type':
'application/json' },
      body: JSON.stringify(newTask),
    })
      .then((response) => response.json())
      .then((data)  =>  setTasks((prevTasks)  =>
[...prevTasks, data]))
```

```
      .catch((error)   =>   console.error('Error
adding task:', error));
  };


  const handleDeleteTask = (taskId) => {


fetch(`https://jsonplaceholder.typicode.com/pos
ts/${taskId}`, {
     method: 'DELETE',
   })
     .then(() => {
       setTasks((prevTasks)                  =>
prevTasks.filter((task) => task.id !== taskId));
     })
     .catch((error)   =>   console.error('Error
deleting task:', error));
  };


  const      handleUpdateTask     =      (taskId,
updatedTitle) => {
    const updatedTask = { title: updatedTitle };


fetch(`https://jsonplaceholder.typicode.com/pos
ts/${taskId}`, {
     method: 'PUT',
     headers:            {           'Content-Type':
'application/json' },
     body: JSON.stringify(updatedTask),
```

```
    })
      .then((response) => response.json())
      .then((data) => {
        setTasks((prevTasks) =>
          prevTasks.map((task) => (task.id ===
taskId ? data : task))
        );
      })
      .catch((error)    =>    console.error('Error
updating task:', error));
  };

  return (
    <div>
      <h1>Task Manager</h1>
      <TaskForm onSubmit={handleAddTask} />
      {loading ? (
        <p>Loading tasks...</p>
      ) : (
        <ul>
          {tasks.map((task) => (
            <li key={task.id}>
              <input
                type="text"
                value={task.title}
                onChange={(e) =>
                  handleUpdateTask(task.id,
e.target.value)
                }
```

227

```
              />
              <button        onClick={()        =>
handleDeleteTask(task.id)}>Delete</button>
            </li>
          ))}
        </ul>
      )}
    </div>
  );
}


export default TaskManager;
```

19.4 Summary of Key Concepts

- **CRUD Operations**: In React, you can perform **Create**, **Read**, **Update**, and **Delete** operations by interacting with external APIs using methods like `fetch()` or `axios`.
- **Forms**: Forms are used to capture user input, which can then be sent to an API to create or update data.
- **State Management**: Use `useState` to manage the data (e.g., tasks) in your React components, and update it accordingly after performing CRUD operations.
- **API Interaction**: Use the `fetch()` function or `axios` to interact with RESTful APIs, handle responses, and manage errors.

19.5 Conclusion

In this chapter, we covered how to handle **CRUD operations** in React using forms to collect user input and interact with external APIs. We also built a **task management app** that allows users to create, read, update, and delete tasks. These concepts are fundamental for building dynamic, data-driven applications in React.

In the next chapter, we will explore **React Hooks** in more detail and learn how to use custom hooks to reuse logic across your components. Let's continue building!

CHAPTER 20

STATE MANAGEMENT WITH REDUX

As React applications grow in complexity, managing state across multiple components can become challenging. While React's built-in state management (`useState` and `useContext`) works well for simple applications, large applications with more complex state interactions require a more structured solution. This is where **Redux** comes into play.

Redux is a state management library that helps you manage **application state** in a centralized store and provides a predictable way to manage state changes in large applications. It is particularly useful for complex applications where multiple components need to share and update state.

In this chapter, we will:

- **Introduce Redux** and understand why it is essential for managing state in React applications.
- Learn about **actions**, **reducers**, and the **Redux store**.
- **Real-world example**: We will build a **shopping cart app** using Redux for state management.

20.1 Introduction to Redux for Complex State Management

Redux is a library that provides a **centralized store** for state management. The state is stored in a single JavaScript object called the **store**. The state can only be modified by dispatching **actions**, which are processed by **reducers** to generate a new state.

Key Concepts of Redux:

1. **Store**: The central place where the application state is stored. The store is an object that contains all the state data for the application.

2. **Actions**: Plain JavaScript objects that describe a change or event in the application. Actions must have a `type` property to specify the type of action being dispatched, and they can also have a `payload` to carry data.

3. **Reducers**: Pure functions that define how the state changes in response to an action. Reducers take the current state and the action as arguments and return a new state.

4. **Dispatch**: A function used to send actions to the Redux store. Dispatching an action triggers the reducer to update the state based on the action type.

20.2 Understanding Actions, Reducers, and the Redux Store

1. The Redux Store

The **store** is where the entire state of your application is kept. It is created using `createStore()` and is the only place where state changes occur in Redux. The store holds the state tree of your application and provides methods to dispatch actions, subscribe to state changes, and retrieve the current state.

```jsx
import { createStore } from 'redux';

const initialState = {
  cart: [],
};

function rootReducer(state = initialState, action) {
  switch (action.type) {
    default:
      return state;
  }
}

const store = createStore(rootReducer);
```

2. Actions

An **action** is a plain JavaScript object that describes the change in the state. It has at least a `type` property, which indicates the action's purpose. Actions can also have additional properties (like `payload`) to carry data that the reducer needs.

Example of a simple action for adding an item to the shopping cart:

jsx

```
const addItemToCart = (item) => {
  return {
    type: 'ADD_ITEM',
    payload: item,
  };
};
```

Explanation:

- The action type (`ADD_ITEM`) describes the type of operation to be performed.
- The `payload` contains the data needed for the operation (in this case, the item to be added).

3. Reducers

A **reducer** is a pure function that defines how the state is updated in response to an action. It takes the current state and an action, and returns a new state. Reducers do not modify the original state; they return a new state object.

Example of a reducer that updates the state based on an ADD_ITEM action:

jsx

```
function cartReducer(state = { cart: [] },
action) {
  switch (action.type) {
    case 'ADD_ITEM':
      return {
        ...state,
        cart: [...state.cart, action.payload],
      };
    default:
      return state;
  }
}
```

Explanation:

- When an ADD_ITEM action is dispatched, the reducer adds the item to the cart array.

234

- The spread operator (`...state`) ensures that we are not mutating the original state but creating a new state object with the updated `cart`.

4. Dispatching Actions

Once we have our actions and reducers set up, we can dispatch actions to the Redux store. To dispatch an action, we use the `dispatch()` method provided by the Redux store.

jsx

```
store.dispatch(addItemToCart({ id: 1, name:
'Apple', price: 1.0 }));
```

Explanation:

- The `dispatch` method sends the action to the Redux store.
- The reducer listens for the action type (`ADD_ITEM`) and updates the state accordingly.

20.3 Real-World Example: Building a Shopping Cart App with Redux

235

Now that we have a basic understanding of how Redux works, let's build a simple **shopping cart app** using Redux. This app will allow users to add, remove, and view items in the shopping cart.

Step 1: Install Redux and React-Redux

First, we need to install `redux` and `react-redux` (the official Redux bindings for React).

bash

```
npm install redux react-redux
```
Step 2: Create the Redux Store and Reducers

We'll create a Redux store to manage the shopping cart state. The state will contain an array of cart items.

cartReducer.js:

jsx

```
const initialState = {
  cart: [],
};

function   cartReducer(state   =   initialState,
action) {
  switch (action.type) {
    case 'ADD_ITEM':
```

```
      return { ...state, cart: [...state.cart,
action.payload] };
    case 'REMOVE_ITEM':
      return {
        ...state,
        cart:      state.cart.filter((item)      =>
item.id !== action.payload.id),
      };
    default:
      return state;
  }
}
```

```
export default cartReducer;
```

store.js:

jsx

```
import { createStore } from 'redux';
import cartReducer from './cartReducer';

const store = createStore(cartReducer);

export default store;
```

Step 3: Set Up React-Redux

To connect Redux with React, we'll use `Provider` to wrap our app and provide the Redux store to all components.

237

index.js:

jsx

```
import React from 'react';
import ReactDOM from 'react-dom';
import { Provider } from 'react-redux';
import App from './App';
import store from './store';

ReactDOM.render(
  <Provider store={store}>
    <App />
  </Provider>,
  document.getElementById('root')
);
```

Step 4: Create the Shopping Cart Component

Now, let's create the ShoppingCart component that will display the items in the cart and allow the user to add or remove items.

ShoppingCart.js:

jsx

```
import React from 'react';
import { useDispatch, useSelector } from 'react-redux';
```

```
function ShoppingCart() {
  const dispatch = useDispatch();
  const cart = useSelector((state) =>
state.cart);

  const addItem = () => {
    const newItem = { id: Date.now(), name:
'Banana', price: 1.5 };
    dispatch({ type: 'ADD_ITEM', payload:
newItem });
  };

  const removeItem = (item) => {
    dispatch({ type: 'REMOVE_ITEM', payload:
item });
  };

  return (
    <div>
      <h2>Shopping Cart</h2>
      <button onClick={addItem}>Add Banana to
Cart</button>
      <ul>
        {cart.map((item) => (
          <li key={item.id}>
            {item.name} - ${item.price}{' '}
            <button onClick={() =>
removeItem(item)}>Remove</button>
          </li>
```

```
    )))}
   </ul>
  </div>
 );
}
```

```
export default ShoppingCart;
```

Explanation:

- We use `useDispatch` to dispatch actions to the Redux store.
- We use `useSelector` to access the current state of the cart from the Redux store.
- The `addItem` function dispatches an `ADD_ITEM` action, and the `removeItem` function dispatches a `REMOVE_ITEM` action.

Step 5: Use the Shopping Cart in the App

App.js:

jsx

```
import React from 'react';
import ShoppingCart from './ShoppingCart';

function App() {
  return (
```

```
<div>
  <h1>Redux Shopping Cart</h1>
  <ShoppingCart />
</div>
  );
}


export default App;
```

20.4 Summary of Key Concepts

- **Redux**: A predictable state container for JavaScript apps, helping you manage state in a more organized way.
- **Store**: The central place where the application's state is stored.
- **Actions**: Plain JavaScript objects that describe the change to be made to the state.
- **Reducers**: Functions that specify how the state should change in response to an action.
- **Dispatch**: The function used to send actions to the Redux store, which then triggers the reducers to update the state.
- **React-Redux**: The official library that provides bindings for using Redux with React.

20.5 Conclusion

In this chapter, we introduced **Redux** as a powerful state management tool for handling complex state in React applications. We explored how to define **actions**, **reducers**, and the **store**. By building a **shopping cart app** with Redux, we demonstrated how to perform basic CRUD operations (add and remove items) in a React application.

In the next chapter, we will explore **performance optimization** techniques in React to ensure your app runs smoothly, even with large datasets. Let's continue building!

CHAPTER 21

OPTIMIZING REACT PERFORMANCE

As React applications grow in complexity, performance optimization becomes essential to ensure that they remain fast and responsive. Even though React is known for its efficiency, improper use of state and rendering can lead to performance bottlenecks, especially with large data sets and complex UI interactions.

In this chapter, we will:

- **Understand performance bottlenecks** in React applications.
- Learn about techniques for optimizing rendering using `React.memo`, `useMemo`, and `useCallback`.
- **Real-world example**: We will optimize the rendering of a large list in a React application to demonstrate how these techniques work in practice.

21.1 Understanding Performance Bottlenecks in React

React is optimized for performance by default, but certain patterns can cause unnecessary re-renders, leading to performance bottlenecks. Common performance issues in React apps include:

1. **Unnecessary Re-renders**: React components may re-render even if their state or props have not changed. This happens when React cannot determine that the component has not actually changed. Re-rendering can be costly, especially when dealing with large components or deep component trees.

2. **Large Lists and Complex Data**: Rendering a large number of items, such as in a list or table, can cause performance issues if not optimized. This happens when React re-renders the entire list every time the state changes, even though only a small part of the list needs to be updated.

3. **Expensive Calculations**: Expensive operations or computations that are run inside render methods or in functions that are frequently called can slow down your application.

4. **Re-rendering Child Components**: If a parent component re-renders, all child components will also re-render by default, even if they don't need to. This can be avoided with the right optimizations.

21.2 Techniques for Optimizing Rendering with React.memo, useMemo, and useCallback

To address performance bottlenecks in React, React provides several tools that help optimize rendering by memoizing components and values.

1. React.memo: Memoizing Functional Components

`React.memo` is a higher-order component (HOC) that wraps a functional component and prevents it from re-rendering if the props haven't changed.

Usage:

```jsx
const   MyComponent   =   React.memo(function
MyComponent(props) {
  // Component code
  return <div>{props.name}</div>;
});
```

Explanation:

- `React.memo` ensures that `MyComponent` will only re-render when its `props` change.

245

- If the `props` stay the same between renders, React will skip rendering the component, saving time and resources.

When to use `React.memo`:

- `React.memo` is most useful when rendering expensive components, or components that render large data sets, where the props don't change often.

2. useMemo: Memoizing Calculated Values

`useMemo` is a hook that memoizes the result of a calculation or function. This is useful for expensive operations that don't need to be recalculated on every render.

Usage:

jsx

```
import { useMemo } from 'react';

function MyComponent({ items }) {
  const sortedItems = useMemo(() => {
    return      items.sort((a,      b)      =>
a.name.localeCompare(b.name));
  }, [items]);  // Only re-calculate if 'items'
change
```

```
return    <ul>{sortedItems.map(item    =>    <li
key={item.id}>{item.name}</li>)}</ul>;
}
```

Explanation:

- `useMemo` will only re-run the sorting operation when the `items` array changes, preventing unnecessary recalculations on every render.
- This is especially useful for expensive operations like sorting or filtering large lists.

When to use useMemo:

- Use `useMemo` when performing expensive calculations in the render cycle, like sorting or filtering large arrays, or doing any computationally expensive operations.

3. useCallback: Memoizing Functions

`useCallback` is similar to `useMemo`, but it is used to memoize functions instead of values. It ensures that the function reference remains stable between renders, preventing unnecessary re-renders of child components that depend on that function.

Usage:

```
jsx
```

```
import { useCallback } from 'react';

function MyComponent({ onClick }) {
  const handleClick = useCallback(() => {
    console.log('Button clicked');
    onClick();
  }, [onClick]);

  return    <button    onClick={handleClick}>Click
me</button>;
}
```

Explanation:

- useCallback ensures that handleClick doesn't get redefined on every render unless the onClick prop changes.
- This is useful when passing functions as props to child components, preventing unnecessary re-renders of those components.

When to use useCallback:

- Use useCallback when you pass functions as props to child components, especially if those child components are wrapped in React.memo, as it prevents the child components from re-rendering unnecessarily due to changes in function references.

248

21.3 Real-World Example: Optimizing a Large List Rendering Application

Let's apply the techniques we've discussed to optimize a large list rendering application. We will simulate a scenario where we need to render a list of items that is large and requires sorting or filtering. Without optimization, this can result in performance bottlenecks when the list is re-rendered unnecessarily.

Step 1: Create a Simple List Component

We will start with a basic list component that renders a large array of items.

jsx

```
import React, { useState, useEffect } from
'react';

function ItemList() {
  const [items, setItems] = useState([]);
  const [filter, setFilter] = useState('');

  useEffect(() => {
    // Simulate fetching large data set
```

```
    const fetchedItems = Array.from({ length:
10000 }, (_, index) => ({
      id: index + 1,
      name: `Item ${index + 1}`,
    }));
    setItems(fetchedItems);
  }, []);


  const filteredItems = items.filter(item =>
item.name.includes(filter));

  return (
    <div>
      <input
        type="text"
        placeholder="Filter items"
        value={filter}
        onChange={(e)                          =>
setFilter(e.target.value)}
      />
      <ul>
        {filteredItems.map(item => (
          <li key={item.id}>{item.name}</li>
        ))}
      </ul>
    </div>
  );
}
```

```
export default ItemList;
```

Explanation:

- This component generates a list of 10,000 items and allows the user to filter them by typing in a search box.
- On every keystroke, the list is filtered and re-rendered, which can be inefficient for large lists.

Step 2: Optimize with useMemo

Now, let's optimize the filtering operation using useMemo. This will prevent unnecessary re-calculations of the filtered list if the filter value doesn't change.

jsx

```jsx
import React, { useState, useEffect, useMemo }
from 'react';

function ItemList() {
  const [items, setItems] = useState([]);
  const [filter, setFilter] = useState('');

  useEffect(() => {
    const fetchedItems = Array.from({ length:
10000 }, (_, index) => ({
      id: index + 1,
      name: `Item ${index + 1}`,
```

251

```
      }));
      setItems(fetchedItems);
  }, []);


  const filteredItems = useMemo(() => {
      return          items.filter(item          =>
item.name.includes(filter));
  }, [filter, items]);


  return (
    <div>
      <input
        type="text"
        placeholder="Filter items"
        value={filter}
        onChange={(e)                          =>
setFilter(e.target.value)}
      />
      <ul>
        {filteredItems.map(item => (
          <li key={item.id}>{item.name}</li>
        ))}
      </ul>
    </div>
  );
}


export default ItemList;
```

Explanation:

- useMemo ensures that the filteredItems array is only recalculated when the filter or items change, reducing the number of re-renders and improving performance.

Step 3: Optimize List Items with React.memo

Now, let's optimize the individual list items by memoizing them with React.memo. This will prevent each list item from re-rendering unless its props change.

jsx

```
const Item = React.memo(({ item }) => {
  return <li>{item.name}</li>;
});

function ItemList() {
  const [items, setItems] = useState([]);
  const [filter, setFilter] = useState('');

  useEffect(() => {
    const fetchedItems = Array.from({ length:
10000 }, (_, index) => ({
      id: index + 1,
      name: `Item ${index + 1}`,
    }));
    setItems(fetchedItems);
  }, []);
```

```
  const filteredItems = useMemo(() => {
    return           items.filter(item        =>
item.name.includes(filter));
  }, [filter, items]);

  return (
    <div>
      <input
        type="text"
        placeholder="Filter items"
        value={filter}
        onChange={(e)                              =>
setFilter(e.target.value)}
      />
      <ul>
        {filteredItems.map(item => (
          <Item key={item.id} item={item} />
        ))}
      </ul>
    </div>
  );
}


export default ItemList;
```

Explanation:

- `React.memo` is used to wrap the `Item` component, ensuring it only re-renders when its `item` prop changes.
- This optimization prevents unnecessary re-renders for each list item.

21.4 Summary of Key Concepts

- **Performance Bottlenecks**: Common performance issues in React include unnecessary re-renders, expensive calculations, and rendering large lists. Optimizing these aspects is crucial for ensuring smooth performance.
- **React.memo**: A higher-order component that memoizes functional components, preventing unnecessary re-renders.
- **useMemo**: A hook that memoizes expensive calculations, improving performance by recomputing values only when necessary.
- **useCallback**: A hook that memoizes functions to ensure their references remain stable across renders, preventing unnecessary re-renders of child components.
- **Optimizing List Rendering**: Techniques like `useMemo` and `React.memo` help optimize the rendering of large lists, making applications more efficient.

21.5 Conclusion

In this chapter, we explored how to optimize performance in React applications using **React.memo**, **useMemo**, and **useCallback**. We applied these techniques to a real-world example of rendering a large list of items in a task management app. By memoizing values and components, we significantly reduced unnecessary re-renders, improving the performance of the application.

In the next chapter, we will dive into **server-side rendering (SSR)** with React to explore how to optimize React applications for faster load times. Let's continue building!

CHAPTER 22

CODE SPLITTING AND LAZY LOADING

As web applications grow in size and complexity, performance optimization becomes critical to ensure users experience fast load times and smooth interactions. One powerful technique for improving performance is **code splitting**, which involves splitting your application's code into smaller, more manageable bundles. This allows you to load only the code that's needed at any given moment, reducing the amount of JavaScript the browser needs to download initially.

In this chapter, we will:

- Explain **code splitting** and why it's essential for large applications.
- Learn how to implement **lazy loading** to load components only when needed, improving performance and user experience.
- **Real-world example**: We will implement lazy loading in a React application to load components only when required, reducing the initial load time.

22.1 What is Code Splitting and Why It's Important for Large Applications?

Code splitting is a technique that breaks down a large JavaScript bundle into smaller, more manageable pieces (chunks). When users visit your application, only the essential code is loaded initially, and additional code is loaded as needed (on-demand).

Why is Code Splitting Important?

1. **Faster Initial Load Time**: By splitting your code, you reduce the size of the initial bundle that needs to be loaded by the browser. This means users can start interacting with your app faster, even on slower networks.

2. **Improved User Experience**: When large applications load everything at once, it can result in a slow initial load time, which can be frustrating for users. Code splitting ensures that users only download the code they need for the part of the app they're interacting with.

3. **On-Demand Loading**: Code splitting enables you to load features only when they are required. For example, you can load the login page only when the user navigates to the login route, rather than loading it upfront.

22.2 Implementing Lazy Loading for Better Performance and User Experience

---

Lazy loading is a technique that allows you to load components or modules only when they are required, instead of loading everything upfront. This approach not only helps with code splitting but also improves performance by reducing the initial load time.

React's Lazy Loading

React provides a built-in function called `React.lazy()` that allows you to implement lazy loading of components. The idea is to import a component only when it's needed, which can significantly reduce the size of the initial bundle.

jsx

```
const MyComponent = React.lazy(() => import('./MyComponent'));
```

This means that **MyComponent** will only be loaded when it is actually rendered for the first time.

Suspense for Fallback UI

When you use `React.lazy()`, you need to handle the case where the component is still being loaded. React provides the `Suspense` component, which allows you to display a loading indicator or fallback content while the component is being loaded.

jsx

```
import React, { Suspense } from 'react';

// Lazy load the component
const    MyComponent    =    React.lazy(()    =>
import('./MyComponent'));

function App() {
  return (
    <div>
      <h1>My React App</h1>
      <Suspense
fallback={<div>Loading...</div>}>
        <MyComponent />
      </Suspense>
    </div>
  );
}
```

Explanation:

- **React.lazy()** is used to lazily load the **MyComponent**.
- **Suspense** wraps the lazy-loaded component and shows a fallback UI (in this case, "Loading...") while the component is being fetched.

Lazy Loading Routes with React Router

React Router works seamlessly with React.lazy() to implement lazy loading of route components. Instead of loading all the routes upfront, you can use React.lazy() to load each route's component only when it's visited.

jsx

```
import React, { Suspense } from 'react';
import { BrowserRouter as Router, Route, Switch
} from 'react-router-dom';

// Lazy load route components
const Home = React.lazy(() => import('./Home'));
const      About      =      React.lazy(()      =>
import('./About'));

function App() {
  return (
    <Router>
      <div>
        <h1>Lazy Loaded React App</h1>
```

```
    <Suspense
fallback={<div>Loading...</div>}>
        <Switch>
          <Route        path="/"          exact
component={Home} />
          <Route                 path="/about"
component={About} />
        </Switch>
      </Suspense>
    </div>
  </Router>
  );
}


export default App;
```

Explanation:

- We use **React.lazy()** to lazy load the **Home** and **About** components.
- **Suspense** wraps the entire Switch component, and the fallback UI ("Loading...") is shown while the required route component is being loaded.

22.3 Real-World Example: Implementing Lazy Loading of Components to Improve App Performance

Let's build a **real-world example** by implementing lazy loading in a **task management app**. We will use lazy loading to load task details only when the user clicks on a task, improving the app's performance.

Step 1: Create the Task List and Task Detail Components
jsx

```
// TaskList.js
import React from 'react';
import { Link } from 'react-router-dom';

function TaskList() {
  const tasks = [
    { id: 1, title: 'Task 1' },
    { id: 2, title: 'Task 2' },
    { id: 3, title: 'Task 3' },
  ];

  return (
    <div>
      <h2>Task List</h2>
      <ul>
        {tasks.map((task) => (
          <li key={task.id}>
            <Link
to={`/tasks/${task.id}`}>{task.title}</Link>
          </li>
        ))}
```

```
      </ul>
    </div>
  );
}


export default TaskList;
jsx


// TaskDetail.js
import React, { useState, useEffect } from
'react';


function TaskDetail({ match }) {
  const [task, setTask] = useState(null);
  const taskId = match.params.id;

  useEffect(() => {
    // Simulate fetching task details
    setTimeout(() => {
      setTask({ id: taskId, title: `Task
${taskId}`, description: `Description for task
${taskId}` });
    }, 1000);
  }, [taskId]);

  if (!task) {
    return <div>Loading task...</div>;
  }
```

```
return (
  <div>
    <h2>{task.title}</h2>
    <p>{task.description}</p>
  </div>
);
}
```

```
export default TaskDetail;
```

Step 2: Implement Lazy Loading for Task Detail Component

In the main app, we will implement lazy loading for the **TaskDetail** component.

jsx

```
import React, { Suspense } from 'react';
import { BrowserRouter as Router, Route, Switch
} from 'react-router-dom';
import TaskList from './TaskList';

// Lazy load TaskDetail component
const    TaskDetail    =    React.lazy(()    =>
import('./TaskDetail'));

function App() {
  return (
    <Router>
      <div>
```

```
        <h1>Task Management App</h1>
        <Suspense
fallback={<div>Loading...</div>}>
          <Switch>
            <Route          path="/"          exact
component={TaskList} />
            <Route             path="/tasks/:id"
component={TaskDetail} />
          </Switch>
        </Suspense>
      </div>
    </Router>
  );
}

export default App;
```

Explanation:

- **TaskList**: Displays a list of tasks with links to their details.
- **TaskDetail**: Displays the details of a specific task. It is lazy-loaded when the user clicks on a task link.
- **React.lazy()**: Is used to lazy load the **TaskDetail** component when the user navigates to a task's page.
- **Suspense**: Wraps the entire routing logic, showing a fallback UI ("Loading...") while the **TaskDetail** component is being fetched.

266

- **Code Splitting**: The process of splitting your application into smaller bundles (chunks) so that only the code necessary for a particular part of the app is loaded.
- **Lazy Loading**: A technique to load components or modules only when needed, reducing the initial load time and improving performance.
- `React.lazy()`: A built-in React function to lazily load components.
- `Suspense`: A component used in conjunction with `React.lazy()` to show a loading indicator while a lazy-loaded component is being fetched.
- **React Router and Lazy Loading**: You can use `React.lazy()` to lazy-load components for specific routes, improving the performance of route-based applications.

22.5 Conclusion

In this chapter, we explored how to optimize React applications using **code splitting** and **lazy loading**. By using `React.lazy()` and `Suspense`, we demonstrated how to improve the

267

performance of React applications by loading components only when needed, reducing the initial load time. This is particularly useful in large applications where some parts of the app are not required immediately.

In the next chapter, we will explore **React's Context API** in more detail, learning how to manage global state across your application without prop drilling. Let's continue building!

CHAPTER 23

HIGHER-ORDER COMPONENTS (HOCS) AND RENDER PROPS

In React, **code reuse** and **component composition** are two key concepts that help developers build efficient and maintainable applications. React provides multiple ways to achieve these goals, and two powerful patterns for doing so are **Higher-Order Components (HOCs)** and **Render Props**. Both patterns allow you to share logic between components in a reusable way.

In this chapter, we will:

- Understand **Higher-Order Components (HOCs)** and **Render Props**.
- Explore how these patterns enhance code reusability and component composition.
- Build a **real-world example** of a reusable **modal component** using HOCs.

23.1 Understanding Higher-Order Components (HOCs)

Higher-Order Components (HOCs) are a pattern in React that allow you to reuse component logic by creating a function that takes a component as an argument and returns a new component with enhanced functionality.

What is an HOC?

An HOC is a function that accepts a component and returns a new component with additional props or behavior. The primary purpose of an HOC is to **reuse component logic** without modifying the original component. HOCs don't modify the original component but rather enhance its functionality by injecting additional props, state, or logic.

Key Characteristics of HOCs:

1. **Takes a component as an argument**: The HOC accepts a component and returns a new component.
2. **Doesn't modify the original component**: It creates a new component that wraps the original one.
3. **Enhances component functionality**: HOCs can add functionality like authentication, data fetching, or UI enhancements.

Basic Example of an HOC:
jsx

```
// HOC that adds a loading spinner to a component
```

```
function withLoading(Component) {
  return    function    WithLoading({    isLoading,
...props }) {
    if (isLoading) {
      return <div>Loading...</div>;
    }
    return <Component {...props} />;
  };
}

function MyComponent({ data }) {
  return <div>{data}</div>;
}

const          MyComponentWithLoading          =
withLoading(MyComponent);

// Usage
<MyComponentWithLoading isLoading={true} />
```

Explanation:

- withLoading is a higher-order component that takes the MyComponent component as an argument and returns a new component that shows a loading spinner while data is being fetched.
- MyComponentWithLoading is the enhanced component that handles the loading state and displays the original MyComponent when the loading is complete.

When to Use HOCs:

- **Code Reusability**: When you need to add the same behavior (e.g., data fetching, authentication) to multiple components.
- **Component Composition**: To create more modular and reusable components by separating concerns.

23.2 Understanding Render Props

The **Render Props** pattern is another approach to code reuse in React. A **render prop** is a function prop that a component uses to know what to render. It allows you to pass a function into a component, and that function returns the component's UI.

What is a Render Prop?

A render prop is a function passed as a prop to a component that gives you access to the component's internal logic, allowing you to decide what should be rendered based on that logic.

Basic Example of Render Props:
jsx

```
function DataProvider({ render }) {
  const data = { name: 'John Doe' };
```

```
  return render(data);
}

function App() {
  return (
    <DataProvider        render={(data)        =>
<h1>{data.name}</h1>} />
  );
}
```

Explanation:

- `DataProvider` is a component that provides `data` to its child components via the `render` prop.
- The `App` component passes a function to the `render` prop of `DataProvider`, which renders the `name` from the data.

When to Use Render Props:

- **Component Flexibility**: When you need to share logic but still want the consumer to control what gets rendered.
- **Dynamic Behavior**: When the component's rendering logic depends on external data or state and needs to be flexible.

273

23.3 How These Patterns Enhance Code Reusability and Component Composition

---

Both **Higher-Order Components (HOCs)** and **Render Props** are designed to enhance the reusability of your React components. These patterns allow developers to:

- **Extract Logic**: Share common logic across multiple components without duplicating code.
- **Increase Flexibility**: HOCs provide a way to add functionality to existing components, while Render Props allow consumers to control what gets rendered while still using the component's internal logic.
- **Improve Composition**: Both patterns allow you to break down complex components into smaller, more focused ones, making your app easier to maintain and scale.

While **HOCs** are great for enhancing or modifying component behavior, **Render Props** are better for controlling what gets rendered, giving you more flexibility and control over the UI.

23.4 Real-World Example: Building a Reusable Modal Component Using HOCs

---

Let's apply these concepts by building a **reusable modal component** that can be shared across different parts of the application. We will use an HOC to enhance the modal component with the ability to show and hide it.

Step 1: Create the Modal Component

First, we'll create a basic modal component that accepts the content to be displayed as a prop.

jsx

```
function Modal({ isOpen, onClose, children }) {
  if (!isOpen) return null;

  return (
    <div className="modal">
      <div className="modal-content">
        <button onClick={onClose}>Close</button>
        {children}
      </div>
    </div>
  );
}

export default Modal;
```

Explanation:

275

- `Modal` is a simple component that shows its children only if the `isOpen` prop is `true`. It also accepts an `onClose` function to close the modal.

Step 2: Create the HOC for Modal

Now, we will create an HOC that enhances the `Modal` component with the ability to control whether the modal is open or closed.

jsx

```jsx
import React, { useState } from 'react';

function withModal(Component) {
  return function WithModal(props) {
    const [isOpen, setIsOpen] = useState(false);

    const openModal = () => setIsOpen(true);
    const closeModal = () => setIsOpen(false);

    return (
      <>
        <Component {...props} isOpen={isOpen}
onClose={closeModal} />
        <button onClick={openModal}>Open
Modal</button>
      </>
    );
  };
```

```
}
```

```
export default withModal;
```

Explanation:

- withModal is a higher-order component that manages the isOpen state (whether the modal is open or closed).
- The openModal and closeModal functions are used to toggle the modal's visibility.
- The HOC wraps the original Modal component and injects the necessary props (isOpen and onClose) to control its behavior.

Step 3: Use the Modal with the HOC

Finally, we use the withModal HOC to create an enhanced version of the Modal component.

```
jsx
```

```
import React from 'react';
import Modal from './Modal';
import withModal from './withModal';

const ModalWithToggle = withModal(Modal);

function App() {
  return (
```

```
<div>
    <h1>HOC Modal Example</h1>
    <ModalWithToggle>
        <h2>Modal Content</h2>
        <p>This    is    a    reusable    modal
component.</p>
    </ModalWithToggle>
    </div>
    );
}


export default App;
```

Explanation:

- `ModalWithToggle` is the enhanced component created by passing the `Modal` component to the `withModal` HOC.
- The modal can now be toggled open and closed by the `App` component, making it reusable across multiple parts of the application.

23.5 Summary of Key Concepts

- **Higher-Order Components (HOCs)**: A pattern that allows you to enhance a component by wrapping it in another function that adds additional functionality, like state or behavior.

- **Render Props**: A pattern that uses a function passed as a prop to determine what gets rendered, providing flexibility and dynamic behavior.
- **Component Reusability**: Both HOCs and Render Props help in writing reusable components by extracting common logic and enhancing component behavior.
- **Code Composition**: These patterns allow developers to break down complex logic into smaller, more manageable pieces, improving code clarity and maintainability.

23.6 Conclusion

In this chapter, we explored **Higher-Order Components (HOCs)** and **Render Props**, two powerful patterns in React that enhance **code reusability** and **component composition**. We learned how to build a **reusable modal component** using both patterns, allowing you to dynamically control component behavior without duplicating code.

In the next chapter, we will explore **React's Context API** in more depth and see how it can be used to manage global state in large React applications. Let's continue building!

CHAPTER 24

ERROR BOUNDARIES IN REACT

In any complex React application, it is inevitable that some components will encounter errors during runtime. These errors can cause unexpected crashes, leading to a poor user experience. To address this, **Error Boundaries** in React provide a way to handle and recover from errors gracefully, without crashing the entire app.

In this chapter, we will:

- **Introduce error boundaries** and understand how they handle JavaScript errors in React apps.
- Learn how to create **custom error boundaries** for better error handling.
- **Real-world example**: We will demonstrate how to use error boundaries to prevent app crashes by adding them to various components.

24.1 Introduction to Error Boundaries

Error Boundaries are a feature in React that allows you to catch JavaScript errors anywhere in the component tree and display a fallback UI, rather than letting the entire app crash.

What Are Error Boundaries?

An **Error Boundary** is a higher-order component that catches errors during the **rendering** process, in **lifecycle methods**, and in **constructor methods** of the components. When an error is caught, React will stop the propagation of the error and display a fallback UI instead of allowing the app to crash.

- **Purpose**: To handle unexpected errors and ensure the app does not crash entirely. Instead, a user-friendly message or alternative UI is shown to the user.
- **Scope**: Error boundaries catch errors in **child components** and do not affect the parent component unless the error boundary itself encounters an error.

When Do Error Boundaries Catch Errors?

1. Errors during **rendering**: Errors that occur while rendering a component's JSX.
2. Errors in **lifecycle methods**: Errors in methods like `componentDidMount`, `componentDidUpdate`, or `getDerivedStateFromError`.

3. Errors in **event handlers**: Errors thrown during event handler execution (though, for event handlers, you will need to use `try/catch`).

Important: Error boundaries **do not** catch errors in:

- Asynchronous code (e.g., in `setTimeout`, `fetch` calls, or promises).
- Server-side rendering (SSR).
- Errors thrown inside **event handlers** (unless explicitly handled with `try/catch`).

24.2 Creating Custom Error Boundaries

To create an error boundary in React, you need to implement the `componentDidCatch()` lifecycle method and the `getDerivedStateFromError()` method. These methods help React catch errors, display fallback UI, and update state when an error is caught.

Basic Structure of an Error Boundary

jsx

```
import React, { Component } from 'react';

class ErrorBoundary extends Component {
```

```
constructor(props) {
    super(props);
    this.state = { hasError: false, errorInfo:
null };
}


static getDerivedStateFromError(error) {
    // Update state to indicate an error has
occurred
    return { hasError: true };
}


componentDidCatch(error, info) {
    // Log the error details for debugging
    console.error('Error    caught    by    Error
Boundary:', error);
    console.error('Error info:', info);
}


render() {
    if (this.state.hasError) {
        return <h1>Something went wrong. Please try
again later.</h1>;
    }


    return this.props.children;  // Render   the
children if no error occurred
    }
}
```

```
export default ErrorBoundary;
```

Explanation:

- **getDerivedStateFromError()**: This method is called when an error occurs and allows you to update the state (e.g., setting hasError to true).
- **componentDidCatch()**: This method provides a way to log the error and additional info, such as where the error occurred in the component tree.
- **Fallback UI**: In the render method, we conditionally render fallback UI (e.g., a message or an alternative component) if an error occurs. Otherwise, we render the children prop, which contains the nested components.

24.3 Real-World Example: Preventing App Crashes by Adding Error Boundaries

---

Let's apply **Error Boundaries** in a real-world React application. We will build a simple app that includes a **Task List** and a **Task Detail** component. We will add an error boundary to prevent the entire app from crashing when an error occurs in any of the components.

Step 1: Create a Task List Component

jsx

```jsx
import React from 'react';
import { Link } from 'react-router-dom';

function TaskList() {
  const tasks = [
    { id: 1, title: 'Task 1' },
    { id: 2, title: 'Task 2' },
    { id: 3, title: 'Task 3' },
  ];

  return (
    <div>
      <h2>Task List</h2>
      <ul>
        {tasks.map((task) => (
          <li key={task.id}>
            <Link
to={`/tasks/${task.id}`}>{task.title}</Link>
          </li>
        ))}
      </ul>
    </div>
  );
}

export default TaskList;
```

Step 2: Create a Task Detail Component

The `TaskDetail` component will display details of a specific task, but we'll intentionally introduce an error in the component to simulate a failure.

jsx

```
import React, { useState, useEffect } from
'react';

function TaskDetail({ match }) {
  const [task, setTask] = useState(null);
  const taskId = match.params.id;

  useEffect(() => {
    // Simulate fetching task data
    setTimeout(() => {
      if (taskId === '2') {
        throw new Error('Failed to fetch task
data'); // Simulate an error for task 2
      }
      setTask({ id: taskId, title: `Task
${taskId}`, description: `Description for task
${taskId}` });
    }, 1000);
  }, [taskId]);

  if (!task) return <div>Loading...</div>;
```

```
  return (
    <div>
      <h2>{task.title}</h2>
      <p>{task.description}</p>
    </div>
  );
}


export default TaskDetail;
```

Explanation:

- We simulate fetching task data with `setTimeout`. If the `taskId` is 2, we throw an error to simulate a failure in data fetching.

Step 3: Create the Main App Component and Wrap with Error Boundary

Now, we will add the `ErrorBoundary` to the main app to catch errors in the `TaskDetail` component.

jsx

```
import React from 'react';
import { BrowserRouter as Router, Route, Switch } from 'react-router-dom';
import TaskList from './TaskList';
```

```
import TaskDetail from './TaskDetail';
import ErrorBoundary from './ErrorBoundary';

function App() {
  return (
    <Router>
      <div>
        <h1>Task Management App</h1>
        <ErrorBoundary>
          <Switch>
            <Route         path="/"         exact
component={TaskList} />
            <Route              path="/tasks/:id"
component={TaskDetail} />
          </Switch>
        </ErrorBoundary>
      </div>
    </Router>
  );
}

export default App;
```

Explanation:

- We wrap the Switch (which contains the routes) with the ErrorBoundary component. This ensures that if any error occurs within the task-related components, the error

288

will be caught by the error boundary, and a fallback UI will be shown.

- If an error occurs in the `TaskDetail` component, such as the simulated error when fetching data for task 2, the app will not crash; instead, the user will see the fallback UI.

24.4 Summary of Key Concepts

- **Error Boundaries**: Error boundaries are components that catch JavaScript errors in their child components and prevent the entire app from crashing. They display a fallback UI instead of breaking the app.
- **Creating Custom Error Boundaries**: Error boundaries are created by defining `getDerivedStateFromError()` and `componentDidCatch()`. These methods handle state updates and log the error details.
- **Fallback UI**: When an error is caught, you can display a fallback UI to the user, such as a friendly error message.
- **Real-World Use**: We used an error boundary to handle errors in a task management app, ensuring that the app didn't crash when there was an error in the task detail component.

24.5 Conclusion

In this chapter, we learned about **Error Boundaries** in React and how they can prevent applications from crashing when errors occur in child components. We built a simple task management app with an error boundary to catch errors in the `TaskDetail` component and prevent the app from crashing. By adding error boundaries, you can improve the resilience of your app and provide a better user experience.

In the next chapter, we will explore **React performance optimization** techniques to ensure your app runs smoothly even with large datasets and complex UIs. Let's continue building!

CHAPTER 25

TESTING REACT APPLICATIONS

Testing is a crucial part of the software development lifecycle. It ensures that your React applications are functioning correctly and helps you catch bugs early, leading to a more stable and reliable product. In this chapter, we will explore the fundamentals of testing React applications, introduce popular testing libraries like **Jest** and **React Testing Library**, and walk through how to write effective unit tests and integration tests for React components.

By the end of this chapter, you'll be able to write tests for your React components and ensure that they work as expected, improving the reliability and maintainability of your application.

25.1 Introduction to Testing Libraries: Jest and React Testing Library

Testing React applications typically involves using a combination of two powerful libraries:

1. **Jest**: Jest is a JavaScript testing framework used to run tests, handle assertions, and provide mock functions. It

comes pre-configured with many features, making it the most popular testing tool for React apps.

2. **React Testing Library**: React Testing Library is designed to help test React components in a way that simulates real-world usage. It encourages tests that focus on the behavior of components and interactions with the DOM, rather than implementation details.

Jest Features:

- **Test runner**: Jest runs your tests and shows results in a clear format.
- **Assertions**: It provides built-in matchers like `expect()` to check if values meet specific conditions.
- **Mocks**: Jest allows you to mock functions, modules, and timers to isolate your tests.
- **Snapshot testing**: Jest can capture a component's rendered output and compare it with a snapshot to detect unintentional changes in the UI.

React Testing Library Features:

- **Focus on user interactions**: React Testing Library encourages testing based on how users interact with the UI (e.g., clicking buttons, typing in inputs).
- **Queries to select elements**: It provides various queries like `getByText`, `getByRole`, and `getByLabelText` to

interact with components in a way that closely resembles how a user would interact with them.

- **Render and cleanup**: It offers utility functions like `render()` to render components and `cleanup()` to remove components after tests are complete.

25.2 Writing Unit Tests for React Components

Unit tests focus on testing individual units of code, typically functions or components, to ensure they work correctly in isolation. In React, unit tests usually verify that a component renders correctly and behaves as expected when interacting with its props or state.

Basic Example: Unit Test for a Simple Component

Consider a simple **UserProfile** component that displays a user's name:

jsx

```
import React from 'react';

function UserProfile({ name, age }) {
  return (
    <div>
```

```
    <h1>{name}</h1>
    <p>Age: {age}</p>
  </div>
 );
}
```

```
export default UserProfile;
```

Now, let's write a unit test to verify that this component renders the user's name and age correctly.

Step 1: Installing Jest and React Testing Library

First, you need to install the necessary dependencies if you haven't already:

bash

```
npm install --save-dev jest @testing-
library/react @testing-library/jest-dom
```

Step 2: Writing the Unit Test

Now, let's write a unit test for the **UserProfile** component using **Jest** and **React Testing Library**.

jsx

```
import React from 'react';
```

```
import { render, screen } from '@testing-
library/react';
import UserProfile from './UserProfile';

test('renders user profile with name and age', ()
=> {
  render(<UserProfile name="John Doe" age={30}
/>);

  // Check if the name is rendered correctly
  const nameElement = screen.getByText(/John
Doe/i);
  expect(nameElement).toBeInTheDocument();

  // Check if the age is rendered correctly
  const ageElement = screen.getByText(/Age:
30/i);
  expect(ageElement).toBeInTheDocument();
});
```

Explanation:

- **render(<UserProfile />)**: This function renders the **UserProfile** component into a virtual DOM for testing.
- **screen.getByText()**: This is a query from **React Testing Library** to select elements based on their text content.
- **expect().toBeInTheDocument()**: Jest assertion to check if the element is present in the DOM.

Step 3: Running the Test

You can run the tests by using the following command:

bash

```
npm test
```

Jest will automatically find and run the tests in files with a `.test.js` or `.spec.js` extension.

25.3 Writing Integration Tests

Integration tests focus on testing how multiple components or pieces of functionality work together. In React, integration tests often verify that components render correctly when provided with data from APIs, or when user interactions trigger state changes in multiple components.

Example: Testing User Profile with API Data

Let's say our **UserProfile** component fetches user data from an API and displays it. We can write an integration test to ensure that the component correctly fetches and displays user information.

jsx

```
import React, { useState, useEffect } from
'react';
import { render, screen, waitFor } from
'@testing-library/react';
import axios from 'axios';

jest.mock('axios');   // Mocking axios for the
test

function UserProfile() {
  const [user, setUser] = useState(null);

  useEffect(() => {
    axios.get('/api/user')
      .then((response)                        =>
setUser(response.data))
      .catch((error)   =>   console.error('Error
fetching user data:', error));
  }, []);

  if (!user) return <div>Loading...</div>;

  return (
    <div>
      <h1>{user.name}</h1>
      <p>Age: {user.age}</p>
    </div>
  );
}
```

297

```
test('fetches and displays user data', async ()
=> {
  // Mock the API call
  axios.get.mockResolvedValueOnce({    data:    {
name: 'John Doe', age: 30 } });

  render(<UserProfile />);

  // Wait for the component to update with the
fetched data
  await  waitFor(()  =>  screen.getByText('John
Doe'));

  // Check if the name and age are displayed
correctly
  expect(screen.getByText('John
Doe')).toBeInTheDocument();
  expect(screen.getByText('Age:
30')).toBeInTheDocument();
});
```

Explanation:

- **jest.mock('axios')**: This mocks the **axios** module, so the actual API call is not made during testing.
- **axios.get.mockResolvedValueOnce()**: This tells Jest to return a resolved promise with mock data for the API call.

- **waitFor()**: This utility from React Testing Library waits for a condition to be true (i.e., the component to update with the fetched data).
- **screen.getByText()**: We use this query to check if the user data is rendered correctly after the API call completes.

25.4 Real-World Example: Writing Tests for a User Profile Component

In this real-world example, we've written both **unit tests** and **integration tests** for a **UserProfile** component. The unit test ensures the component correctly displays the passed-in name and age. The integration test verifies that the component can fetch user data from an API and display it.

Step-by-Step Testing Recap:

1. **Unit Tests**: Write tests to check that components render correctly with given props.
2. **Integration Tests**: Write tests to verify that components interact correctly with external data or APIs.
3. **Mocking**: Use Jest's mock functionality to mock APIs or functions during tests.

These practices ensure that your components work as expected, and changes to one part of the application don't unexpectedly break other parts.

25.5 Summary of Key Concepts

- **Jest**: A JavaScript testing framework used for running tests and handling assertions.
- **React Testing Library**: A library focused on testing React components by simulating user behavior and interacting with the DOM.
- **Unit Tests**: Tests focused on verifying individual components' behavior and functionality.
- **Integration Tests**: Tests that ensure different parts of the application, such as components and APIs, work together.
- **Mocking**: The process of replacing real API calls or functions with mock implementations during tests.

25.6 Conclusion

In this chapter, we introduced the basics of testing React applications using **Jest** and **React Testing Library**. We covered how to write **unit tests** to verify that individual components render correctly and **integration tests** to ensure that components interact with external APIs as expected. By writing tests for your components, you can ensure that they behave correctly, reducing bugs and improving the overall stability of your app.

In the next chapter, we will explore **end-to-end testing** with tools like Cypress and Selenium to simulate real user interactions across your entire app. Let's continue testing and improving!

CHAPTER 26

DEPLOYING REACT

APPLICATIONS

Once you've built a React application, the next crucial step is deploying it so that users can access it over the web. Deploying a React app involves preparing it for production, choosing a deployment platform, and configuring it for optimal performance.

In this chapter, we will:

- **Prepare React applications** for production deployment.
- Explore **deployment tools** like **Netlify**, **Heroku**, and **AWS** for deploying your app.
- Walk through a **real-world example** of deploying a React app to **Netlify**, one of the most popular platforms for hosting static websites.

26.1 Preparing React Applications for Production Deployment

Before deploying your React app, there are several steps you need to take to ensure that it is optimized for production. This includes building the app, minifying JavaScript and CSS, and optimizing images and assets.

Step 1: Build the React App for Production

React provides a built-in tool to bundle your application for production using **Webpack**. This bundling process creates an optimized version of your app, which is smaller in size and faster to load.

To prepare your app for production, run the following command:

```bash

npm run build
```

Explanation:

- The `build` script creates a **build/** folder that contains a production-ready version of your app.
- This production build includes:
    - **Optimized JavaScript**: The JavaScript is minified and optimized for performance.
    - **Minified CSS**: The CSS files are minified, reducing their size.
    - **HTML File**: A single HTML file that loads your app's bundled JavaScript and CSS files.

    o   **Source Maps**: These are optional and helpful for debugging in production. You can choose to exclude them in the production build for security reasons.

Step 2: Test the Production Build Locally

Once the build is ready, it's important to test it locally before deploying to ensure everything works as expected.

You can serve the production build locally using the `serve` package:

1. First, install `serve` globally:

    bash

    ```
    npm install -g serve
    ```

2. Then, serve the build folder:

    bash

    ```
    serve -s build
    ```

3. Visit `http://localhost:5000` to see your app running in production mode.

This ensures that the production build works as expected on your local machine before going live.

There are several platforms available to deploy your React application. Here, we will discuss three of the most popular options: **Netlify**, **Heroku**, and **AWS**.

1. Deploying to Netlify

Netlify is one of the easiest and most popular platforms for deploying React applications, especially for static sites. Netlify provides continuous deployment, automatic HTTPS, and a simple configuration.

Steps to Deploy a React App to Netlify:

1. **Create an Account**: Go to Netlify and sign up for an account (you can sign in using GitHub, GitLab, or Bitbucket).
2. **Push Your Code to GitHub**: Ensure your React app is version-controlled using Git and pushed to a repository on GitHub.
3. **Connect Your Repository to Netlify**:

- o Go to the **Netlify Dashboard** and click **New Site from Git**.
- o Choose your Git provider (e.g., GitHub), authenticate, and select the repository containing your React app.
- o Set the build settings:
  - **Build command**: `npm run build`
  - **Publish directory**: `build`

4. **Deploy**:
   - o Netlify will automatically build and deploy your app. After a few seconds, your React app will be live with a unique Netlify domain (e.g., `your-app.netlify.app`).

5. **Custom Domain**: You can also add your own custom domain to the app through the Netlify dashboard.

Why Choose Netlify?

- **Automatic Deployments**: Netlify integrates directly with GitHub and automatically deploys your app whenever you push changes to your repository.
- **Fast and Free**: Netlify offers fast deployments, continuous integration, and a free tier with generous limits.

2. Deploying to Heroku

Heroku is another platform that offers cloud application hosting, and it is commonly used for deploying full-stack applications, including React apps with a backend. You can deploy a React app on Heroku by serving it with a server like **Express**.

Steps to Deploy a React App to Heroku:

1.   **Set Up Express Backend**:
     o   If your React app doesn't already have a backend, create a simple **Express server** that serves the React build.

```javascript
const express = require('express');
const path = require('path');

const app = express();

// Serve static files from the React app
app.use(express.static(path.join(__dirnam
e, 'build')));

// Handle all requests to React app
app.get('*', (req, res) => {
  res.sendFile(path.join(__dirname,
'build', 'index.html'));
```

307

```
});

const PORT = process.env.PORT || 5000;
app.listen(PORT, () => {
  console.log(`Server is running on port
${PORT}`);
});
```

2. **Create a `Procfile`**:
   - In the root of your project, create a file named `Procfile` (with no extension) and add the following line:

```
bash
```

```
web: node server.js
```

This tells Heroku to start the **Express server** when your app is deployed.

3. **Push Your Code to GitHub**: Ensure your code is pushed to a GitHub repository.

4. **Deploy to Heroku**:
   - Log in to Heroku and create a new app.
   - Connect the Heroku app to your GitHub repository.
   - Enable automatic deployments or manually deploy your app from the Heroku dashboard.

5. **View Your App**: After the deployment process, Heroku will provide a URL where you can view your app.

Why Choose Heroku?

- **Backend Support**: Heroku is ideal if you have a full-stack app with both a React frontend and a backend (e.g., Express or Node.js).
- **Easy to Use**: Heroku offers simple deployment via Git and integrates well with GitHub.

3. Deploying to AWS (Amazon Web Services)

For more complex applications or production-level apps, **AWS** offers powerful infrastructure and deployment options, including **S3** (for static sites) and **EC2** (for full-stack apps). Deploying to AWS requires a bit more configuration but provides scalability and flexibility.

Steps to Deploy a React App to AWS S3:

1. **Build the React App**:
   - Run `npm run build` to create a production build.
2. **Set Up AWS S3 Bucket**:
   - Log in to AWS and create an **S3 bucket**.
   - In the **Bucket Settings**, enable **Static Website Hosting**.

309

o Upload the contents of your **build/** folder to the S3 bucket.

3. **Set Permissions**:
   o Make the bucket public so that the files can be accessed by users.
   o Set the appropriate **bucket policy** to allow public access.

4. **Access Your App**:
   o Once uploaded, you will get an S3 endpoint URL (e.g., `http://your-bucket-name.s3-website-us-east-1.amazonaws.com`) to access your app.

Why Choose AWS?

- **Scalability**: AWS provides robust infrastructure for scaling your application as your user base grows.
- **Flexibility**: AWS offers a wide range of services for various deployment needs, including static and dynamic hosting.

26.3 Real-World Example: Deploying a React App to Netlify

Let's take a simple **React Todo List app** and walk through the deployment process to **Netlify**.

1. **Build the App**: Make sure your app is production-ready by running the build command:

```bash
```

```
npm run build
```

2. **Push Your Code to GitHub**: Ensure your app is version-controlled with Git and pushed to a repository on GitHub.

3. **Sign Up for Netlify**: Go to Netlify and sign up (you can use your GitHub account).

4. **Connect GitHub Repository to Netlify**:
   o Click **New Site from Git**.
   o Select **GitHub** and authorize Netlify to access your repository.
   o Choose the repository containing your React app.

5. **Configure Build Settings**:
   o **Build command**: `npm run build`
   o **Publish directory**: `build`

6. **Deploy the Site**: Click **Deploy Site**, and Netlify will automatically build and deploy your React app. You will receive a public URL like `your-app.netlify.app`.

7. **Custom Domain (Optional)**: You can also set up a custom domain (e.g., `www.yourwebsite.com`) through the Netlify dashboard.

26.4 Summary of Key Concepts

- **Preparing for Production**: To deploy a React app, first run `npm run build` to create an optimized version for production.
- **Deployment Platforms**: Platforms like **Netlify**, **Heroku**, and **AWS** provide different hosting solutions for React applications.
- **Netlify**: Easy and fast deployment for static sites. Supports automatic deployment from Git.
- **Heroku**: Ideal for full-stack applications with a backend. Supports Node.js, Express, and other backend technologies.
- **AWS**: Powerful and scalable cloud infrastructure, ideal for enterprise-level applications or complex deployments.

26.5 Conclusion

In this chapter, we explored how to **deploy React applications** to popular platforms such as **Netlify**, **Heroku**, and **AWS**. By following the deployment process, you can ensure your React app is live and accessible to users. Netlify is particularly great for static websites, while Heroku and AWS offer more robust solutions for full-stack applications.

In the next chapter, we will explore **React performance optimization** techniques to make sure your deployed app runs smoothly, even under heavy user load. Let's continue building!

CHAPTER 27

FINAL PROJECT: BUILDING A FULL-STACK REACT APPLICATION

In this final chapter, we will consolidate everything we've learned throughout the book by building a **full-stack React application**. Full-stack development involves combining a **frontend** (React), a **backend** (Node.js/Express), and a **database** (MongoDB or PostgreSQL) to create a fully functional web application.

For this example, we will build a **to-do application** that allows users to add, edit, and delete tasks. The frontend will be developed using **React**, while the backend will be powered by **Node.js/Express**, and we will use **MongoDB** as the database to store the tasks.

This project will give you a comprehensive understanding of how to connect the various pieces of a full-stack application and deploy it to the web.

27.1 Overview of Full-Stack Development

Full-stack development involves building both the **client-side (frontend)** and **server-side (backend)** components of a web application, as well as the **database** that stores and retrieves data.

- **Frontend (React)**: The user interface that users interact with. It communicates with the backend through HTTP requests (typically using REST APIs).
- **Backend (Node.js/Express)**: The server-side logic that handles requests from the frontend, performs business logic, and interacts with the database.
- **Database (MongoDB/PostgreSQL)**: The database stores application data, such as user information or to-do tasks.

In this chapter, we will walk through building and deploying a **full-stack to-do app**, which will cover the following components:

1. **Frontend**: Building the React app.
2. **Backend**: Setting up a Node.js/Express server with RESTful API routes.
3. **Database**: Integrating MongoDB (or PostgreSQL) to store the to-do tasks.
4. **Deployment**: Deploying the application to a platform like Heroku and MongoDB Atlas (or using PostgreSQL on Heroku).

315

27.2 Setting Up the Backend (Node.js/Express)

Step 1: Create the Backend Project

1. **Initialize a new Node.js project**:

   bash

   ```
   mkdir todo-backend
   cd todo-backend
   npm init -y
   ```

2. **Install necessary dependencies**:

   bash

   ```
   npm install express mongoose cors dotenv
   ```

   o **express**: Web framework for Node.js.
   o **mongoose**: ODM (Object Data Modeling) library to interact with MongoDB.
   o **cors**: Middleware to enable Cross-Origin Resource Sharing (CORS) for requests from the frontend.
   o **dotenv**: Used to manage environment variables.

3. **Create the server**: In the `todo-backend` directory, create a file named `server.js`.

```
js

const express = require('express');
const cors = require('cors');
const mongoose = require('mongoose');
const dotenv = require('dotenv');

dotenv.config();

const app = express();

// Middleware
app.use(express.json());
app.use(cors());

// Database connection
mongoose.connect(process.env.MONGO_URI, {
useNewUrlParser: true, useUnifiedTopology:
true })
  .then(() => console.log('Connected to
MongoDB'))
  .catch((error) => console.log('MongoDB
connection error:', error));

// Basic route
app.get('/', (req, res) => {
  res.send('Welcome to the To-Do API');
});
```

```
// Listen on port
const PORT = process.env.PORT || 5000;
app.listen(PORT, () => {
  console.log(`Server is running on port
${PORT}`);
});
```

- o This server listens for HTTP requests and connects to MongoDB using Mongoose.

Step 2: Set Up the To-Do Model

In models/Task.js, create a schema for the to-do tasks.

js

```
const mongoose = require('mongoose');

const taskSchema = new mongoose.Schema({
  text: {
    type: String,
    required: true
  },
  completed: {
    type: Boolean,
    default: false
  }
});

const Task = mongoose.model('Task', taskSchema);
```

318

```
module.exports = Task;
```

Step 3: Create the API Routes

In the `routes` folder, create a file named `tasks.js` for handling the CRUD operations (Create, Read, Update, Delete).

```js
const express = require('express');
const router = express.Router();
const Task = require('../models/Task');

// Create a new task
router.post('/tasks', async (req, res) => {
  const { text } = req.body;
  const task = new Task({ text });

  try {
    const savedTask = await task.save();
    res.status(201).json(savedTask);
  } catch (error) {
    res.status(400).json({          message:
error.message });
  }
});

// Get all tasks
router.get('/tasks', async (req, res) => {
```

319

```
  try {
    const tasks = await Task.find();
    res.status(200).json(tasks);
  } catch (error) {
    res.status(500).json({                message:
error.message });
  }
});


// Update a task
router.patch('/tasks/:id', async (req, res) => {
  try {
    const            task            =           await
Task.findById(req.params.id);
    task.completed = req.body.completed;

    const updatedTask = await task.save();
    res.status(200).json(updatedTask);
  } catch (error) {
    res.status(400).json({                message:
error.message });
  }
});


// Delete a task
router.delete('/tasks/:id', async (req, res) =>
{
  try {
    await Task.findByIdAndDelete(req.params.id);
```

```
    res.status(200).json({      message:      'Task
deleted' });
  } catch (error) {
    res.status(500).json({                 message:
error.message });
  }
});
```

```
module.exports = router;
```

Step 4: Integrate Routes with the Server

In `server.js,` import and use the tasks routes.

```
js
```

```
const tasksRoutes = require('./routes/tasks');
```

```
app.use('/api', tasksRoutes);
```

27.3 Setting Up the Frontend (React)

Step 1: Create the React App

1. Create a new React app using `create-react-app:`

   ```bash
   ```

   ```
   npx create-react-app todo-frontend
   ```

```
cd todo-frontend
```

2. Install Axios for making HTTP requests:

```bash
bash
```

```
npm install axios
```

Step 2: Create the To-Do Components

Create a component for displaying and managing the to-do tasks.

TaskList.js (to list tasks):

```jsx
jsx
```

```jsx
import React, { useState, useEffect } from
'react';
import axios from 'axios';

function TaskList() {
  const [tasks, setTasks] = useState([]);

  useEffect(() => {

axios.get('http://localhost:5000/api/tasks')
      .then((response)                         =>
setTasks(response.data))
      .catch((error) => console.error(error));
  }, []);
```

```
  const handleDelete = (id) => {

axios.delete(`http://localhost:5000/api/tasks/$
{id}`)
      .then(() => setTasks(tasks.filter((task)
=> task._id !== id)))
      .catch((error) => console.error(error));
  };

  return (
    <div>
      <h2>Task List</h2>
      <ul>
        {tasks.map((task) => (
          <li key={task._id}>
            {task.text}
            <button          onClick={()          =>
handleDelete(task._id)}>Delete</button>
          </li>
        ))}
      </ul>
    </div>
  );
}

export default TaskList;
```

AddTask.js (to add tasks):

```
jsx
```

```
import React, { useState } from 'react';
import axios from 'axios';

function AddTask() {
  const [text, setText] = useState('');

  const handleSubmit = (e) => {
    e.preventDefault();


axios.post('http://localhost:5000/api/tasks', {
text })
      .then((response) => {
        console.log('Task            added:',
response.data);
      })
      .catch((error) => {
        console.error('There was an error adding
the task:', error);
      });
  };

  return (
    <form onSubmit={handleSubmit}>
      <input
        type="text"
        value={text}
```

```
        onChange={(e)                         =>
setText(e.target.value)}
        placeholder="Enter a task"
        required
      />
      <button type="submit">Add Task</button>
    </form>
  );
}


export default AddTask;
```

Step 3: Combine Components

In `App.js`, combine `TaskList` and `AddTask` to manage the to-do tasks.

jsx

```
import React from 'react';
import TaskList from './TaskList';
import AddTask from './AddTask';


function App() {
  return (
    <div>
      <h1>To-Do App</h1>
      <AddTask />
      <TaskList />
    </div>
```

```
  );
}
```

```
export default App;
```

27.4 Deploying the Full-Stack Application

Step 1: Deploying the Backend to Heroku

1. Create a **Heroku app**:

   bash

   ```
   heroku create
   ```

2. Set up MongoDB on **MongoDB Atlas**:
   - Create a free cluster on MongoDB Atlas and get the connection string.
   - Update your .env file in the backend with the MongoDB URI:

     env

     ```
     MONGO_URI=your-mongodb-uri
     ```

3. **Deploy** your backend to Heroku:

   bash

```
git push heroku master
```

Step 2: Deploying the Frontend to Netlify

1. Push your frontend code to GitHub.

2. Create a **Netlify** account and connect it to your GitHub repository.

3. Deploy the app using **Netlify**:

   o In Netlify's dashboard, select the GitHub repository and deploy it.

   o Configure the build settings:

      ▪ **Build command**: `npm run build`

      ▪ **Publish directory**: `build`

4. After deployment, your app will be live on **Netlify**!

27.5 Summary of Key Concepts

- **Frontend**: React is used for the user interface, interacting with the backend via API calls.

- **Backend**: Node.js and Express are used to handle requests, perform CRUD operations, and interact with the database.

- **Database**: MongoDB (or PostgreSQL) is used to store and retrieve data.

- **Deployment**: We deployed the backend to **Heroku** and the frontend to **Netlify** for a fully functional web application.

27.6 Conclusion

In this final chapter, we built a **full-stack to-do application** using **React**, **Node.js/Express**, and **MongoDB**. We learned how to create a backend that handles data, a frontend that communicates with the backend, and how to deploy both to the web using **Heroku** and **Netlify**. This comprehensive project gives you the foundation to build and deploy full-stack applications, from simple CRUD apps to more complex systems.

With the skills you've gained, you're ready to tackle real-world projects and deploy them with ease. Keep practicing, building, and experimenting to deepen your understanding of full-stack development. Happy coding!

www.ingramcontent.com/pod-product-compliance
Lightning Source LLC
LaVergne TN
LVHW051431050326
832903LV00030BD/3019